A Jewish Journey

Surviving and Thriving in Poland, Israel, and the United States

Samuel M. Ron
With Caren Schnur Neile

HAMILTON BOOKS
AN IMPRINT OF
ROWMAN & LITTLEFIELD
Lanham • Boulder • New York • London

Published by Hamilton Books
An imprint of The Rowman & Littlefield Publishing Group, Inc.

4501 Forbes Boulevard, Suite 200, Lanham, Maryland 20706
www.rowman.com

86-90 Paul Street, London EC2A 4NE, United Kingdom

British Library Cataloguing in Publication Information Available

Library of Congress Cataloging-in-Publication Data

Names: Ron, Sam, 1924– author. | Neile, Caren S., author.
Title: A Jewish journey : surviving and thriving in Poland, Israel, and the United States / Sam Ron—with Caren Schnur Neile.
Description: Lanham, Maryland : Hamilton Books, an imprint of Rowman & Littlefield, [2023] | Summary: "Never forget. This stirring memoir of Polish Holocaust survivor Samuel Ron is structured as a Q&A with students, in order to reflect the decades he has spent educating groups about his survival from four Nazi concentration camps, and his many contributions to the founding of the modern State of Israel"—Provided by publisher.
Identifiers: LCCN 2022039713 (print) | LCCN 2022039714 (ebook) | ISBN 9780761873587 (paperback) | ISBN 9780761873594 (epub)
Subjects: LCSH: Ron, Sam, 1924—Miscellanea. | Holocaust survivors—Poland—Miscellanea. | Holocaust, Jewish (1939–1945)—Poland—Miscellanea. | Holocaust survivors—Israel—Miscellanea. | Holocaust survivors—United States—Miscellanea.
Classification: LCC DS134.72.R665 A3 2023 (print) | LCC DS134.72.R665 (ebook) | DDC 940.53/18092—dc23/eng/20220824
LC record available at https://lccn.loc.gov/2022039713
LC ebook record available at https://lccn.loc.gov/2022039714

∞™ The paper used in this publication meets the minimum requirements of American National Standard for Information Sciences—Permanence of Paper for Printed Library Materials, ANSI/NISO Z39.48-1992.

A Jewish Journey

For my beloved family: especially my wife, Bilha, our children and their children, our parents, my brother, and for all those who can no longer speak for themselves.

Thus says the Lord God; Come from the four winds, O breath, and breathe upon those slain, that they may live.

—Ezekiel 37:9

Contents

Foreword

Elie Wiesel often attested that he did not want to be the last Holocaust survivor. The burden of the past threatens to crush those living in the present. Sam Ron's remarkable autobiography tells this nearly 100-year-old survivor's story. Far from being crushed by the past, Mr. Ron began his post-War life with a determination to both thrive and continue his Jewish legacy. Jewish culture has historically responded to tragedies with stories: tales that affirm life even in the face of death. From biblical times, through rabbinic Judaism, from the Hasidic tradition to contemporary times, historic catastrophes have produced both lamentation literature and tales of hope and remembrance. It is as if collectively the Jewish people have embraced the biblical injunction to choose life over death.

In this fascinating life story, Polish-born Samuel Ron, a witness to the greatest tragedy to have befallen the Jewish people, shares his story with Professor Caren Schnur Neile. Fittingly, their intergenerational encounter, which reflects the questions students have asked Sam over the years, links the biblical commandment to remember with the survivor's obligation to bear witness. Through their question and answer format, the events of seventy-plus years ago become part of contemporary culture.

Although Sam Ron is no longer able to participate in the annual March of the Living events, and his public speaking appearances have had to be curtailed, his recall of the horrors of the Holocaust and the acts of the few righteous gentiles he encountered remain vivid in his memory. Together with his wife Bilha, Sam remains committed to bearing witness. His presentations have moved generations of students to enquire about the contemporary lessons and legacies of the Holocaust. Sam's experiences have served to reinforce his strong sense of Jewish identity. They serve a similar purpose among the students fortunate enough to have heard and been influenced by his testimony.

This memoir is a model of how the generations can communicate about the past and move knowledgeably into the future. Caren Neile reveals the importance of careful listening and the willingness to ask questions that reside at the heart of any meaningful dialogue. Issues of identity, persistence and refusal to despair are all strong elements of this memoir. This is not to claim that Sam Ron was callous or indifferent toward his Holocaust experience. Quite the opposite is true. He has lived in Europe, Israel, and America. He is fully aware of history's vicissitudes. But Sam Ron is not a victim. He is a proud survivor.

Alan L. Berger, Ph.D.
Raddock Family Eminent Scholar Chair in Holocaust Studies
Director, Center for the Study of Values and Violence After Auschwitz
Florida Atlantic University
Affiliated Professor of the University of Haifa

Introduction

Man's Search for Listeners

Caren Schnur Neile

In his masterwork *Man's Search for Meaning*, the psychiatrist and Holocaust survivor Viktor Frankl notes that in psychoanalysis, "the patient must lie down on a couch and tell you things which sometimes are very disagreeable to tell."[1] According to Frankl's own therapeutic approach called logotherapy, conversely, "the patient may remain sitting erect but he must hear things which sometimes are very disagreeable to hear."

Rereading this passage while working with Samuel Ron on his memoir puts me in mind of Ron's forty-year career in informal Holocaust education. If, in keeping with Frankl's conception of logotherapy, the primary goal for human beings is not pleasure, as Freud argued, but rather meaning, then it appears that Ron has long since reached his goal. He has found his life's meaning at least in part by recounting his experiences during the Holocaust to those who were ready to hear some very disagreeable things—as well as listen. There is, of course, a distinction between the two activities. Most of us can't help hearing; after all, we are born with two open ears. It's the listening—the belief that "attention must be paid,"[2] as Miller wrote with respect to his hapless salesman—that isn't always so readily available.

Hearing and listening are the wellspring of *A Jewish Journey*, because Ron's particular gift of meaning-making has been most evident in his use of the oral tradition, the form of communication that has sustained for millennia not only Jews—as evidenced, for example, by the religious and cultural importance of "*Torah sheh b'al peh*"[3] and the seminal prayer known as "the Shema"[4]—but also every culture on Earth. Ron's use of orality takes the form of witness testimony.[5] As far as effective witnesses go, he checks off all the boxes. An effective witness must have a good memory. Check. Something to say. Check. A balance of right-brain/left-brain skills to simultaneously evoke emotion and organize content into a narrative that exhibits coherence and fidelity.[6] Charisma also helps. So does a genuine need to be listened to, and a platform through which to speak. Check, check, check again.

Born Shmuel Rakowski in Kazimierza Wielka, Poland, Ron suffered a similar fate to that of Frankl during the Holocaust, the Nazis' systematic attempt during World War II to obliterate European Jewry, in addition to homosexuals, the disabled, and others. Unlike Frankl, however, Ron went on to become a builder and developer, living a comfortable life in Israel and the U.S. in relative obscurity, until, that is, he found his public voice. It has been my privilege to listen as Sam Ron recounted his life story to me for this book. Thousands more have experienced his testimony in synagogues and lecture halls, and at the site of monuments, mass graves, and former concentration camps. Some have even witnessed his witnessing in the front yard of his childhood home in Poland. For all these people in all these places, Ron's oral testimony has been perhaps as important a form of meaning-making as it has for Ron himself.

THE POWER AND PROMISE OF WITNESS TESTIMONY

Oral testimony takes many forms, including statements provided in a formal setting such as a court of law, and, in the Christian evangelical tradition, descriptions of the process by which an individual found God. In addition to the well-known trials related to the Holocaust, since the 1970s, people have also testified about their experiences both as perpetrators and victims of human rights abuses in Truth and Reconciliation Commissions.

In all these situations, the power of showing up, of physical presence, is palpable. Beyond the myriad benefits of live interaction between witness and audience is an added sense that witnesses quite literally stand (or sit) behind their words. Looking someone in the eye, hearing their voice and seeing their face and body language provides an element of somatic data that contributes to judgments as to the veracity and sincerity of the speaker. Can an in-person witness lie? Indubitably. Is it harder to do so than on paper? Certainly.

THE HOLOCAUST WITNESS

> Sam Ron is an extraordinarily credible witness. When he delves into his memory and retrieves the various accounts of his life during the Holocaust he creates a visual that just mesmerizes listeners. I have had the occasion to listen to him recount the events that affected his and his family's lives and watch how

> the youngsters are enraptured with his recitation. . . . the stories come alive. . . . Everyone who listens to Sam is taken by him and falls in love with this amazing survivor. I have known Sam for twenty-seven years, and each time I hear him retell his story it's almost like hearing it for the first time. . . . [7]

Survivors of the Nazis' genocidal campaign have often said that they believe they escaped death in order to serve as witnesses for those who did not. And yet not so long ago, there existed a mere handful of Holocaust memoirs. Just as writing follows speaking in human development, so did Holocaust memoir begin with the oral narrative tradition. Before that, for many survivors, came silence. Only a few, such as Elie Wiesel in 1956, Primo Levi in 1947, and the same year, on behalf of his daughter Anne, Otto Frank, had published accounts of their experiences by the 1950s.

For many others, the same held true for speaking. Until the Eichmann Trial, the Holocaust played little if any part in public, or even private conversation. Even in Israel, a new nation forming its identity after the war, many survivors were loathe to share their stories for fear of being labeled "sheep that went meekly to the slaughter," or else "*sabon*," Hebrew for *soap*, a reference to the use to which the Nazis were said to have put Jewish body fat. In the United States, survivors were often disbelieved, ignored, or outright shunned. Gurewitsch notes:

> The eyewitnesses . . . who had encountered ignorance of and indifference to their experiences, were wary of sharing memories that brought them pain and nightmares. Would they be believed now, after such a long time? When they first arrived in the US as refugees after World War II their need to tell about their experiences was met with disbelief and insensitivity. "We had a hard time here during the war; sugar was rationed," and "Forget about the past; get on with your life" were typical reactions of American families and acquaintances.[8]

Echoing this sentiment, Ron told me that many survivors did not want to talk because people did not want to hear. Beyond refraining from speaking to the public, some never spoke of their experiences even to each other. In explanation he asks rhetorically: What was there to say?

Then, in large part in response to the publication of a book by a Holocaust denier, the four-part mini series *Holocaust* aired to record audiences in 1978, and the floodgates of Holocaust memories started to swing open. Increasingly, survivors spoke more openly about their war experiences at houses of worship, commemorative community events, Jewish organizations, schools, and other venues. What is more, many did so in print. By 2001, an editor at a university press told me that so many memoirs had been written by Polish survivors in particular that a manuscript had to have something extra special, such as an unusual writing style or exotic locale, to find a publisher. In other words, Polish survivors' stories were no longer news.

Twenty years later, a recent search of the term "Holocaust memoir" on amazon.com yields over 4,000 results. It is impossible to say how many more than 4,000, because "over 4,000" is all that the site reveals. At one point in 2015, that number was exactly 3,369.[9] How did this happen? For one thing, survivors know that time is running out. For another, although it may be more difficult for a non-professional writer to publish a memoir with a traditional publisher, the explosion of self-publishing has encouraged many survivors and their families to pay to see their life stories in print, if only for family and friends.

Thus we have, it seems, come full circle. The war ended seventy-seven years ago. Now, the difficulty is finding people to *tell* their stories. As two South Florida TV reporters discussed with Ron on International Holocaust Remembrance Day this year, not only are fewer survivors alive, but also far fewer are able to speak to the public about their experiences. Sam Ron is one of the last Holocaust witnesses.

PROCESS AND PRODUCT

> We were touring Auschwitz when somebody made a nervous joke in my hearing. I turned around to see, and when we made eye contact, all the blood drained from the poor boy's face.
>
> "Don't worry!" I said, loud enough so that others could hear. "You know by now that I make plenty of jokes myself. . . . You can laugh; you can say what you want. All I ask is that you listen and learn. If you listen, I will be happy. That's why I'm here." (Page 149, this book)

I wrote earlier of meaning-making in Ron's testimony. Allow me to be more specific. Sam Ron's participation in the ritual of testifying is no less than an act of social action. He leads the audience through Victor Turner's stages of the social drama: breach/crisis/redress and integration or schism.[10] They are, as has been suggested (e.g., Schechner),[11] the same elements found in testimony. When listeners have moved through each stage, they are transformed, as the celebrant is in any ritual. And what is effective social activism if not transformative?

Unfortunately, Samuel Ron cannot continue to participate in this ritual for another 50 years. When World War II ended, he was just twenty-one years old. At this writing, he is nearly 98. He appears quite healthy, and he is still able to tell his story in person and for various media companies. But even the few survivors born in camps are now at least seventy-seven years old, and they have no firsthand memories of the war years. Ron himself has had to curtail his speaking schedule recently, and not only as a result of the pandemic. Due to his advanced age, he can no longer qualify for the required insurance to participate in the March of the Living educational travel program that has been so important to him and his listeners.

This dearth of survivors presents a growing problem for Holocaust educators, who long relied on the live testimony of eyewitnesses to instill a sense of urgency to the encomium "Never again." When Rabbi Weissberg wrote about Ron, he based his comments on a longstanding professional relationship that is ebbing away, even as young people are faced with growing challenges to their Jewish identities. A book is undoubtedly a more lasting legacy—if it is read.

A Jewish Journey therefore follows a structure that is different from typical Holocaust memoirs. Because it is based on the oral testimony of a man who has so often and so successfully spoken to groups, and because his most urgent request to his audiences is that they listen, Ron and I chose as the book's format an imaginary Q&A that in fact reflects many of the questions students ask him.

Then there is the form the responses take. On the opening page of their anthology of female survivor testimony, Rittner and Roth[12] present a poem by survivor Gertrud Kolmar called "The Woman Poet." They draw special attention to the poem's final line, "You hear me speak, but do you hear me feel?" I too am drawn to that line, because I am intensely aware of the challenge of the listener's stance. When we witness the witnesses, we may be tempted to fool ourselves into thinking that the storyteller's story is *our* story, or that, at the very least, we fully understand it. On Passover, Jews are encouraged to feel as though we were personally brought out of Egypt, along with the Hebrew slaves. And yet we were not slaves. That is to say, we can take in the words, but can we take in the feelings?

To respond to that question, I created this book, with Sam Ron's blessing, in a vivid narrative style. It does not simply take the form of his straightforward oral history, that is, a lightly edited transcript of his spoken presentations. Without his smile, his voice, his gestures, his presence—without the full oral narrative "package"—his words are not quite as evocative, particularly to a younger audience. Thus this book is an attempt to shape witness testimony into a set of readable set pieces. That is to say, stories.

One definition of story is shaped, sequential evocation of experience that evokes emotion, and with it learning, understanding and identification. Emotion is story's stock-in-trade. Since the time of Plato, it has been understood that emotion heightens memory and learning. Sam Ron can effectively tell his own story live because he is a warm, articulate, credible witness.[13] This is no easy task. A ghostwriter's job is to climb behind the eyes and inside the hearts of her subjects, attempt to bring to life on the page what they have seen and felt, and submit the result to them for correction. All of which leads to the question: In this era of contested truths, shouldn't it matter whether or not the exact dialogue that was spoken is reproduced on the page, or the correct color of the dress or hair of a character? I suggest that as long as the reader is informed of the process—that Sam's story is true to the best of his prodigious memory—it should not. This memoir is not a work oral history. It is a work of memory and emotion.

SOME FINAL THOUGHTS

Samuel Ron has been a participant in the two defining moments of modern Jewish history, both the most tragic and the most triumphant. Thus I would be remiss if I did not mention a large part of his story: his experiences in pre-1948 Eretz Yisrael, and his role in the founding of the State of Israel. When he served as an educator for the March of the Living, Ron was as much in demand when speaking during the tour in Israel as he was during the week in Poland. Such *chalutzim*, as the early pioneers are called, are nearly as rare these days as are Holocaust survivors, particularly in the U.S. And yet, their heroic contributions—among other accomplishments Ron helped found a kibbutz and was wounded in battle—changed lives. These stories too must be shared by the witnesses.

Years ago, I had the privilege of participating, with Rabbi Leon Weissberg at the South Palm Beach County JCC, in the first U.S. program of Witness Theater. Created in Israel, Witness Theater brings together survivors and teens to bond, share stories, and create a production in which the young people embody some of the survivors' experiences onstage. While facilitating this program, I saw firsthand how the survivors felt not just heard, but also listened to, and how the children learned.

Nevertheless, as Weissberg points out with respect to March of the Living, even a few days after meeting a survivor, the intensity of the experience for teens begins to dampen.[14] How much were the young participants still influenced by the program a year, five, ten years later? Did they still "hear" the feelings? Although I am certain they did initially, I can imagine that other feelings and thoughts and experiences overtook them. That is the way of the human brain and the human heart. I suggest that just as with the Torah, which is read each week in the synagogue, or the Seder and every other ritual, Jewish or not, we must continue to renew the connection to Sam Ron and other survivors and chalutzim, to continue to listen, and never stop hearing them feel. As Rittner and Roth[15] write:

> Gertrud Kolmar's life and especially her question "But do you hear me feel?" echo protest and even resistance. Her question is the right one. . . . Listening for that question, hearing it, heeding it, responding to it—those acts could lead us, as the poet urges, to change our minds, to wake ourselves, and to move in ways that mend the world.

It is my fervent hope that Sam Ron's book, like his life's work, help effect that transformation. I have been extremely fortunate to have played a part.

In the Afterword to the 2006 edition of Frankl's seminal work,[16] William J. Winslade recounts that the eminent psychoanalyst was once asked to write in one sentence the meaning of his own life. Then he asked his college students to guess what he wrote. One guessed it correctly.

"The meaning of your life," the student said, "is to help others find the meaning of theirs." In a sense, the same could be said for any effective witness. But none has done that for me and for so many others more than Sam Ron.

"Listen!" wrote the young Thereisenstadt poet Alena Synkova. "Now it's time."[17]

NOTES

1. Victor Frankl, *Man's Search for Meaning* (Beacon Press, 1946/2006), 98.

2. Arthur Miller, *Death of a Salesman* (Viking Press, 1949).

3. Oral law, the sacred oral tradition that complements the Torah, codified in the Talmud.

4. Literally, "hear," from the infinitive "l'shmoa." "L'hakshiv" is the infinitive of "listen."

5. Many similarities exist between witness testimony and the art of confessional, or personal storytelling, and at times I conflate the terms. However I privilege "witness testimony" due to some of the negative implications, particularly in an age of Holocaust denial, of the term *storytelling*.

6. Walter Fisher. Narrative as a Human Connection Paradigm: The Case for Public Moral Argument. *Communication Monographs*, *51,* no.1(1984): 1–22.

7. Leon Weissberg, email correspondence, January 2022.

8. Brana Gurewitsch, ed. *Mothers, Sisters, Resisters: Oral Histories of Women Who Survived the Holocaust* (University of Alabama Press, 1998).

9. Leon Weissberg and Caren Schnur Neile. Never Forget: March of the Living and Place-Based Holocaust Storytelling. *Storytelling, Self, Society*, *11,* no. 1(2015): 121–136.

10. Victor Turner. *The Ritual Process: Structure and Anti-Structure* (Aldine de Gruyter, 1969).

11. Richard Schechner. *Between Theater and Anthropology* (University of Pennsylvania Press, 1985).

12. Carol Rittner and John Roth. *Different Voices: Women and the Holocaust* (Paragon House, 1998).

13. In fact, he may need to. Storytellers internalize the stories they tell, which, in the case of difficult stories, can be an extremely stressful and difficult enterprise. Imagine reliving a traumatic event over and over again for decades.

14. Weissberg, Neile, 2015.

15. Rittner and Roth, (1993, 16).

16. William J. Winslade, Afterword. In Victor Frankl, *Man's Search for Meaning* (Beacon Press, 2006).

17. A. Synkova, "To Olga." In Hana Volavkova, . . . *I Never Saw Another Butterfly . . . Children's Drawings and Poems from Terezin Concentration Camp 1942–44.* (1962) Second Edition. McGraw-Hill. n.p.

Timeline

1924	Born Shmuel Rakowski, July 28, Kazimierza Wielka, Poland, to Sofia and Jozef Rakowski
1939	Nazis enter Kazimierza Wielka, went into hiding in Boszczynek
1941	Arrived in Krakow Ghetto
1942	Sent to Plaszow
1943	Sent to Pionki
1944	Sent to Sachsenhausen
1944	Sent to Glowen subcamp
1945	Death March, liberation, reunited with mother in Krakow
1946	Joined Bericha, reunited with father in Austria, arrived in Eretz Yisrael
1947	Met Bilha Zehori, joined Haganah, went to Nevatim
1948	State of Israel declared
1949	Married Bilha, changed last name to Ron
1950	First child Tamar born
1951	First visit to the U.S.
1952	Moved to Kfar Saba, Israel
1954	Second child David born
1955	Moved to Tel Aviv
1956	Went to Canton, Ohio, to visit, ended up staying in the U.S.

1957	Moved to Akron, Ohio
1961	Third child Daphnae born
1969	Parents died
1970	Returned to Canton
1974	Moved again to Israel
1975	Returned to Canton
1980	First trip to Poland, with son David
1989	Second trip to Poland, with Bilha
1995	First of eleven March of the Living trips, with Canton group
1998	Bought winter home in Boca Raton, Florida
2004	Moved to Boca Raton full-time
2016	Sold businesses, moved to Sinai Residences on JCC Campus in Boca Raton
2019	Final March of the Living trip

PART I

The Talk

The sleek black limousine pulled up to the Sinai Residences porte-cochère that morning in the winter of 2018 with the controlled purr of a tame tiger. Living in what was billed as "an upscale independent senior living community" in Boca Raton, Florida, the building's residents were not unused to luxury. But a private limo at ten in the morning was undoubtedly VIP service, and more than one curious onlooker waiting for their Lexus at the valet station surveyed the entranceway for the intended passenger. When the parting lobby doors emitted a blast of cool air, followed by Sam Ron, five-foot-eight and ninety-three years old, no one was particularly surprised.

Sam hadn't always been a celebrity. As a successful developer back in Canton, Ohio, he was often overshadowed by his wife Bilha, a brilliant and popular educator. Born in the Land of Israel before it became a country, Bilha had her own story to tell. But Sam had lived through the Krakow ghetto and the Nazi death camps. And with every passing year, fewer of his fellow survivors were around to share their experiences with young people, and to admonish them that never again should human beings treat each other with such inhumanity. This message, he believed, was becoming increasingly urgent as the numbers of witnesses diminished.

A gregarious man, Sam usually began to kibitz with the driver from the moment he stepped into the car. But this time, he was lost in thought. A local high school principal had just essentially told a student's mother that the Holocaust was a "belief" rather than a fact. How could one man combat such ignorance, he wondered. Where will it end?

"I see I'm taking you to that fancy private school," the driver said suddenly, glancing at his phone and then at the rearview mirror. "You got a grandchild going there or something?"

Sam shook his head. "I'm a speaker. They've brought me in to talk to the children."

"Oh yeah?" The driver, well used to chauffeuring older people, hadn't counted on a man with a mission. "What do you talk about? Health? The old days, maybe?"

"I talk about the Holocaust." Sam had been looking out the window; now he faced the dyed blond head of the man in front of him. "You know what is the Holocaust?"

He had expected the pause that followed. Even from people who knew exactly what the Holocaust was, there was always an inevitable moment when that beat, that intake of breath and exhalation of curiosity, came to the surface. He was a walking piece of history, and he didn't mind the response to that fact in the slightest. In fact, he welcomed it.

"Yeah, I think we learned about that in school. The Germans, right? And what they did to Jewish people. You Jewish, sir?"

"I am. Do you know any Jews?"

"Around Boca? Is the Pope Catholic?" He laughed.

So the young man knew something about the subject, although Sam wondered how much. Twenty-five years earlier, the Florida Legislature had passed the Holocaust Education Bill, requiring every school to teach the Nazi reign of terror. Due to its large Jewish population, Florida is one of just a handful of states requiring K-12 genocide education and maintaining a state commission or task force to keep the curriculum comprehensive and up to date.

He could see by the narrowing eyes in the mirror that the driver was preparing to ask another question. What would it be? Had he been in the camps? Yes. Did he lose family? Yes. Was it horrible? Yes, yes, yes.

The chauffeur took a breath, and so did Sam. "Well," the young man asked at long last. "You want to take the Turnpike or I-95?"

In the post-rush hour traffic, the ride to Fort Lauderdale took just over half an hour. The gleaming morning sun couldn't penetrate the tinted window to Sam's left; still he liked knowing it was there. It was nice to be in Florida in the winter. And when the limousine dropped him off at the four white pillars marking the school's curved driveway, he happily breathed in the Florida air, humid though it was. He was prepared for the routine that followed, having done it so many times before. As always, a small phalanx of faculty, parents and students ushered him in to breakfast as if he were a rock star. Some of the teenagers pelted him with questions; their voices shaking and breaking with a mix of hormones and nervousness.

One slight, dark-haired boy in a knitted blue yarmulke called out to him, "Mr. Ron, do you still believe in God after what happened to you?"

Sam pursed his lips. He beckoned the boy closer so he didn't have to shout.

"Well, I tell you," he said, "different survivors reacted in different ways. I consider myself a religious person, but I go to a Reform temple, which means it's not very strict when it comes to observing the commandments. But your question of what I believe, that's controversial, and I don't think it's right to discuss it here. All I can tell you is, I don't blame God for the bad in this world or credit Him for the good. He does what He does."

The boy frowned, nodded, and melted into the crowd.

One or two others held out notebooks and pens.

Sam shook his head. "What's this?"

"Will you give us your autograph?" a heavyset girl asked.

This was a new one. He raised his eyebrows.

"Who do you think I am, Clark Gable?"

One of the parents laughed. "I don't think she knows who that is, Mr. Ron. But I see the resemblance!"

Others, too shy perhaps to approach, simply stared, or smiled, or both. After the simple meal, a parent and teacher stayed behind with him in the room along with a single class of twenty-one young people. The students eyed him in hushed silence.

The teacher gave a brief introduction, then Sam rose to approach the lectern. He knew that the teens had been primed for his talk, and that his strong accent and intense topic would encourage them to focus on every word. He also knew what they would respond to. How it felt to be hungry, not just for lunch, but really starving, for eight months. What it was like to ride in airless, stuffed cattle cars without knowing if you were traveling to your death. Having no idea what had happened to your family for months, or years, on end. He was glad that he had such exceptional communication skills. How else would a bunch of healthy Florida teenagers grasp the meaning of hell?

He took a deep breath and began, providing some background, telling some of his stories. Before long he saw the tears spilling along downy cheeks; he heard the quiet sobs. He glanced at the teacher, who nodded. This was to be expected. They would deal with it.

He concluded his talk, and the room was pin-drop silent. This used to bother Sam, but now he was used to it. After a minute or so, and after a standing ovation, he asked for questions. What were they still wondering about? What had really touched or hurt them? What was it they still needed to know?

PART II

The Questions and Answers

Chapter 1

What Was It Like for You as a Boy in Poland?

"Hey, Rakowski! Dirty Jew!"

It was an epithet I had heard directed to others, but never to me. All I knew about anti-Semitism in our little Polish village of Kazimierza Wielka was what we'd seen and heard happen to others. The ugly name-calling, particularly around Easter. The sections of town where we weren't welcome. The boycotting of Jewish-owned businesses. The authorities even assessed our taxes at a higher rate than they did the non-Jews.

That morning I had been sitting in my fifth-grade classroom, minding my own business. That wasn't easy with fifty other boys and girls around me, many of them shoving and giggling and chatting when the teachers' backs were turned. I liked school, and I did well. I remember I was doing the writing assignment the head teacher had given us, dipping my pen into the inkwell each time it ran dry, as people used to do before the invention of ballpoint and fountain pens. Scratch, scratch, scratch a few lines, then dip. Scratch, scratch, scratch, then dip again. In more modern parts of Poland, in the big cities of Warsaw and in nearby Krakow, the inkwell had already pretty much fallen out of use by 1934. It was an indication of just how backward our village still was, despite the big new school building and the modern sugar factory.

Maybe the Jew-haters had left me alone because our family, which had been in town for generations, owned a lumberyard, and we were respected for that, and for the electricity that our major client, the sugar factory, connected to our house. Maybe it was the fact that unlike the two other Jewish kids in school, whose first language was Yiddish, I spoke perfect Polish, because my parents used it regularly in business. Maybe it was because our family wasn't so religious, although we did keep kosher and observe the holidays. I didn't have to wear a yarmulke, or *payos*, those curled earlocks that some Jewish boys hid behind their ears when they went out into the Gentile world.

We were Jews, sure, but we didn't look and act as different from the others as some of our people did.

Whatever the reason, I knew my family was lucky. I had heard my parents talk about what was going on in next-door Germany, where the Nazis made anti-Semites feel increasingly easy about speaking against Jews and inciting violence. I also knew it could happen here, too. Just because our town was named after the 14th-century King Kazimierz III, who was relatively good to the Jews, that didn't mean that we were safe. (*Wielka* means "big" in Polish, by the way. The nearby town was Kazimierza Mala, for "small.") Although Jews had lived in Poland nearly a thousand years, they were often merely tolerated, and sometimes not even that. There were four main areas of town—the Gentile farms, the sugar factory with all its buildings, the estate of the great nobleman Lubinski, and the Jewish quarter—and our kind wasn't welcome at every gathering in the first three. In our town of 3,000, maybe only sixty families were Jewish. After all, Poland was a Catholic country.

I looked up at the cross on the schoolroom wall, and I thought of the prayers I had heard the priests lead that morning. I knew them well, because although they taught religion in school only on Saturdays, when we Jews were home for our Sabbath, the Catholic prayers were said every morning. *Hail Mary, full of Grace*. I could recite it in my sleep. Theirs was supposed to be a religion of love, but the Church taught that Jews had killed Jesus, and that we used Gentile children's blood to make our matzoh on Passover. What could I, little Shmuel Rakowski, do to combat all that propaganda? And why should I try?

Dirty Jew!

Every student and teacher was looking at me, waiting to see what I would do. Our head teacher was known as the biggest anti-Semite in town; the head of them all, although he had always been good to me, his best student. Now I could feel his eyes piercing my skin. Still, no one's pricked me more than those of the two Jewish girls who kept to themselves in the back of the room, Bella Weiczenberg and the Oshinski girl. How was I going to react? Would I just take it, like so many of our people, young and old, did all the time, had done through casual humiliations and murderous pogroms for centuries?

I was not a big kid, but I had confidence, even then. My parents had instilled pride in my little brother Yulik and me. Even at that young age, I knew who I was. I was the eldest son of the most prominent Jews in town, respected for their successful business and connections. My father was an ardent Zionist, believing that the Jews deserved our own country in Eretz Yisrael. During elections for the Zionist Congress, our home was a nest of activity, meetings and papers and a whole big to-do.

I remembered the little I had heard about my namesake, my mother's father Shmuel Menachem, whom I had never known. What would make him proud? I thought of the movies—of course still black-and-white and silent in those days—that I went to in our town, with heroes like John Gilbert and Douglas Fairbanks. Should I cower, or should I fight? If I fought back, would I get punished, even though I was justifiably defending myself? Would I get hit with a baseball bat, like they did to the kids who got in trouble in *cheder*? But if I did nothing, how would I feel about myself? And would they ever leave me alone?

All this sounds like I deliberated for hours, but really it took seconds for me to make up my mind. I thought of a line from the Hail Mary prayer I had heard just that morning: *Pray for us sinners, now and at the hour of our death.* Then I reached out to the hole in my wooden desk to pick up the inkwell, which was the size of a small coffee cup. Without a moment's hesitation, I tipped it over the kid's head.

As I did, I yelled out, "Look who's dirty now!"

The room, which has been buzzing like a hive moments before, was suddenly silent. Nobody moved. Everyone stood paralyzed as the black viscous fluid slithered from my tormentor's spiky blond hair to his shocked face and down half of his white shirt.

I held my breath.

And then, as if on cue, the room exploded into applause and cheers. Even the head teacher had an expression of pure delight on his face as he handed the filthy boy to his assistant to take out of the room.

"Get him cleaned up, will you?" he asked, barely able to contain his laughter.

For the rest of the day, students from that class and others—because in a small town news spreads like a virus—came up to congratulate me, or just looked at me in astonishment from afar, whispering to their friends and pointing.

"Did you hear what he did? Shmuel Rakowski!"

After class let out for the day, I made my way home among the horses and buggies, past the butcher, the tailor, the restaurants, bars, drugstore, synagogue, churches, even the bagel maker from out of town, who, I am willing to swear, made the best egg bagels on the planet, brown as pretzels and sweet as sugar beets. It was a Monday, and the women were doing their shopping in the *rynek*, hair wrapped in colorful scarves, wearing skirts and work boots; the children were playing in the street. Farmers and horse traders, merchants of every kind, called out to the passing customers, hawking their wares.

With all that tumult, it should have come as no surprise that the news of my altercation preceded me back to our new, two-story, red wooden house with the large white windows, right on the main street of Sienkiewicza in the

Jewish section, adjacent to the lumberyard. With nine people in our home including my aunt and uncle, cousins and grandmother, there was always somebody home. And if not, I could always go to one of the many households in town to which I was related, with twenty-six first cousins.

When I stopped outside to get a drink of water from the well, my mother emerged from the front door to greet me. She was a modern woman, a very practical and matter-of-fact businesswoman, not given to huge displays of emotion.

"Shmulik," she said simply, as I came toward her. To my surprise, she took me in her arms and kissed my forehead.

"Your father and I are very proud of you. Everyone deserves to be treated with respect. You showed them that."

"I wasn't very respectful when I poured that ink," I said with a grin.

With a shrug, she turned toward the door, a smile playing on her lips.

"I was born in this town," she said. "So was your father, and both our mothers. To live here, we do what we have to do. Whatever happens to us in the future, I know you will survive."

I was still too young at the time to know exactly what she was referring to, but I knew it sounded good.

Chapter 2

Can You Describe the Time Leading Up to War?

I stared at my reflection in the tailor's mirror and felt my heart pound. Sure I had had a Bar Mitzvah, the Jewish ceremony of manhood, the previous year. Yes, I was growing taller, and my voice and face were beginning to change. Like others my age, I carefully nurtured the first few hairs of adolescence on my face. But this was different. I could hardly believe that at age fourteen, I was a man at last, wearing the dark blue uniform of my soon-to-be high school in Krakow, after having completed the compulsory Polish education up to seventh grade in my town. I puffed out my thin chest. I adjusted the cap, its school number shining. I stood tall and proud. The girls, Jewish and not, were already starting to look at me in the street. Now they were going to be so impressed!

On my arrival to the busy city a few weeks later, I felt as though I'd landed in heaven, rather than a place about thirty miles from my home. Catching sight of my reflection in the train window, I had to remind myself more than once to close my gaping mouth. Situated on the Vistula River, Krakow is a beautiful place. It is one of the oldest cities in Poland, dating back well over a thousand years, and also the second largest, next to Warsaw. Everywhere I looked were majestic old buildings, greenery on the streets and in the magnificent park, and people dressed in what to my village eyes, at least, looked like the most sophisticated finery.

Apart from the many yeshivas, there were four Jewish high schools in Krakow, one general, one vocational, one just for girls, and the one I was going to, specializing in business. I wasn't sure what I wanted to do with my life, but I figured that as the elder son, maybe I'd eventually take over the family lumberyard. It was fine by me. I wanted to be a *macher*, like my father before me. And I hoped to have some fun doing it.

Whatever I chose to do, since there were no high schools in my town, I had had a great excuse to move to the big city. As an added bonus, just down the road from Stradom No. 10, on the main street where the high school was situated, was the home of my mother's kind and beautiful younger sister Sarah Levenstein, her husband Isaac, and my cousins Esther and Shmuel Menachem, named just like me. (Every firstborn son in my mother's family had that name.) So I was all set up with a convenient and comfortable place to live.

Walking to class through the Old City that first day, I passed the Jewish section of town, Kazimierz—familiar, no?—with its Yiddish theater and, across the street from the school, the Atlantic Cinema, where the famous radical Zionist Zev Jabotinsky would come to speak the following year. Next door to the school was the Polish Army headquarters. How important we were!

I had always done well in school, and that didn't change. I can honestly say I loved being in high school. And I enjoyed everything else the city had to offer a young man. Living with the Levensteins combined the best of being an elder son and an honored guest. My aunt treated me like the favorite nephew I was, and her two kids looked up to me like a big brother. Plus, although we weren't allowed to be seen in it on the streets of Krakow, I wore that crisp uniform home for visits whether I had to or not, because the ways the girls flirted with me was worth the little bit of discomfort. It was, all in all, a good life.

Then, on November 10 of that year, 1938, I woke to the horrified faces of my aunt and uncle. The entire Jewish community was terrified. The date of November 9 came to be known as Kristallnacht, the Night of Broken Glass, when German-Jewish shopkeepers saw their store windows explode into shards at the hands of a mob; when synagogues, schools and homes were vandalized, one hundred Jews were killed, and 30,000 of our people deported to concentration camps.

Because we were still relatively safe in Poland, once many of them were expelled, the Polish Jews in Germany came to us. When the authorities housed the refugees in the student union hall of our high school, we students talked of little else. Who would be next? What were the Nazis planning? My friends and I walked through Stradom debating the issues, trying to feel secure in the knowledge that Berlin was far away, nearly 400 miles from Krakow.

But there was still happiness to be had, and when Chanukah came around that winter, I was honored with the task of blessing the candles at the Jewish theater.

Baruch atah adonai, eloheynu melech ha'olam, asher kidishanu b'mitzvotav, v'tzivanu, l'hadlik nayr, shel Chanukah.

Baruch Atah Adonai, eloheynu melech ha'olam, sheh asah nisim lavotaynu, ba'yamim, ha hem, ba z'man ha zeh.

> Blessed art Thou oh Lord our God, King of the Universe, who makes us holy through your commandments and commands us to light the Chanukah candles.
>
> Blessed art Thou oh Lord our God, King of the Universe, who made miracles for our ancestors in their days at this season.

It was a holiday of miracles, which meant that anything was possible, and I continued to feel like a million. Oh I heard the nervous discussions of the adults, sure. But I, Shmuel Rakowski, didn't have a care in the world. Still, I knew others around me were suffering. The students at the local Polish Jagielonski, or Jagellonian University, were famously anti-Semitic, making Jewish students sit in the back, or, if they refused to do that, stand. The student were always getting into fights with the Jewish kids, as well as with Jews who just walked by and were too dumb, or brave, to avoid the luxurious plantings that obscured violence from public view. How do I know? Because sometimes my friends and I would go there on purpose, looking for trouble. What can I say? There was something deeply satisfying about defending myself, about sticking it to the anti-Semites. After all, at least in high school, I was a man in uniform!

Things went on like that for the entire school year. By the summer of 1939, however, Germany had already annexed Czechoslavakia, and the tension was rising between Germany and Poland. I heard about it, of course, but by then the family lumberyard took all my attention. That summer, my father sent my mother and Yulik to the Tatra mountains as usual, but I stayed with him and worked. And boy, did I work! I got to know a little about the two trucks that we owned with some other Jewish businesses, hand-pumping the gas because the town had no electricity for the gas tanks. I also checked on the sawmills that we leased in Rakow and Kurozweki, supervising or actually doing the bookkeeping myself. These towns were far enough away from mine that I had to stay there for weeks at a time, but by then I was comfortable being away from home. I boarded with the bookkeeper in Kurozweki, and with a stranger in Rakov.

One night, the bookkeeper and I were talking over dinner.

"Things are looking bad for the Jews in Germany and Czechoslovakia," I said. "Let's see what the Polish Army does if they come here."

"You know what Marshal Rrydz-Smigli says," he replied, shaking his head. Edward Rrydz-Smigli was a general, second in authority to the President. "He won't give up one button to the Germans!"

I had to laugh. "You know what my parents say? He won't give one button, but they'll take the whole coat!"

We could make jokes; everything was happening so far away, and we were young and doing fine. But then it was August, and Germany demanded an open corridor straight through to Danzig, which today is called Gdansk. The bookkeeper sat me down with his family and talked to us about how to put on gas masks, how to tape the windows, everything we would need to know to protect ourselves from what everyone saw as the coming war.

By the end of the month, the Army called up the reservists and requisitioned the lumberyard trucks. Without those trucks, I had a hard time getting back home from the sawmills, more than fifty miles away. The trains were brimming with soldiers. Between the bus and my own two feet, I finally made it by the end of the month.

My mother, as I've said, was a practical woman. After greeting me and commenting on how good I looked, she said, "We don't know what's coming, Shmuel. I have to stock up on more flour and potatoes. And be sure to get to the tailor to get your school uniform fitted. You've grown like a weed!"

I remember standing in that tailor shop for the second time, admiring my reflection from all sides. What would the girls in town think of me now, a year older, when I came home by train wearing this uniform?

I never had the chance to find out.

Chapter 3

How Did War Come to Your Town?

The roar of the German bombs dropping over Warsaw, even though it came from many miles away, reached us like the fury of a thousand lions, swooping down from the sky, claws unfurled. It was September 1, 1939, 5 a.m. Waking to the tumultuous dawn, I had my first sleep-addled thought: that these were in fact our own Polish planes.

"We're fighting the Germans!" I told my brother. "They won't stay for long, you'll see."

But my father shook his head. "That's not the sound of Polish aircraft," he said quietly. "That's the German Luftwaffe." In time, I was to hear those sleek, buzzard-like fighter jets in my dreams.

It wasn't a total surprise; still, no one knew what to think. This was Friday, the day to prepare for *Shabbos*, the Jewish day of rest. But instead of quietly checking off their weekly to-dos, making cholent and challah or cleaning the house, people were on the streets and in the stores in a state of panic. Everyone was scrambling for staples, and we too grabbed all the flour and sugar we could find. We knew that thousands of Jews and Poles were fleeing the capital. Where would they go, if not to small towns like ours?

"Don't worry how much you spend," my father told my mother. "With the Germans here, our money will probably be worthless before long anyway." Then his gaze fell on her gold earrings.

"Give me those, Sophie," he said, holding out his hand. "And any other jewelry you've got. I'm going to find a good hiding place for it." My mother grew pale with worry, but I was merely curious.

"Hiding place?" I asked, as she quickly removed her few good pieces and ran off searching for more.

"Son," he said grimly, "it's only a matter of time before the Germans reach us here in Kazimerza Wielka."

His words seemed to freeze in the crisp air. I could only imagine the worst, so I tried to simply focus my mind on the logistics of preparation. What would we need? What could I do to help? Until then, I had been mainly content to be a kid, but now, I wished with all my being that I were older.

By Sunday, my father and some of the other younger men were ready to flee for the East, figuring they would be safer there, at least for a while. At the door, my mother looked at him searchingly.

"When will we see you again?" she whispered.

He took her hands in his. "Don't worry about me, Sophie. I'll just be gone till we know what's what. As for all of you," he looked around at the household, "I've arranged for you to go to the Molendas' basement at the slightest sign of trouble. They told me they'd be glad to take you in. We can trust them."

"Why the Molendas?" Even in time of strife, I was such an inquisitive kid. Why go next door, I wondered, when it would be quicker to hide where we were? And why to one of the biggest anti-Semites in town?

"Because they've got a brick house right on the street," my uncle said before my father could open his mouth. "It'll be safer there. And we'll be able to see what's going on." When he saw my face, he added, "The Molendas may not like Jews, but they've always been fair to us. At this point, they're the best option we've got. It's a good thing they're willing to help."

I nodded. That made sense to me. Our wooden house was set back from the street, behind the lumberyard. So no one would see us flee. And ur neighbors owned a bar and restaurant, which meant that we would have no shortage of food if we needed to stay there a while. Still, the thought of running outside during an invasion was to keep me up that night, as well as the next. When my father left, I wanted to hug him for all I was worth. But that was not our way. Instead, I said goodbye and told him I'd see him soon. For the rest of the evening we sat around, not speaking much, unable to focus on anything. We all went to bed early.

And then, just three mornings after the first bombs dropped in Warsaw, we were sitting at breakfast when we heard the crack of gunfire. It didn't sound so far away. We exchanged frightened looks, but no one said a word. We all dropped our forks and cups, grabbed a few items of clothing and a bit of food, and took off for the basement next door. The Molendas were already there, seated knee-to-knee in the dusky light. I waved half-heartedly to Janina, their pretty daughter who was in my class. She smiled thinly and looked away.

Crouching in the opposite corner alongside my grandmother and my uncle's family, my mother held Yulik and me close. Like my friends, I usually tried to keep my little brother at a distance, though I did look out for him when he needed me. Not only was he three years younger, but he was also a bit of a mama's boy. That day, however, even though I was fifteen years old and a high school student, I was so terrified that I welcomed the security of those familiar bodies. For a little while, it felt good to be a kid.

Soon, however, the noise outside got so loud that I had to see what was going on, and I made my way to the windows facing the street, careful to stay out of sight of any passersby. There, just a few feet away, were the tanks, trucks, armored cars and soldiers of the most threatening army I could imagine, like something out of a nightmare. To my horror, I watched as our Polish cavalry horses galloped as fast as their horrified riders could coax them—in the opposite direction.

When I came back and reported what I'd seen, my grandmother, who had lived through the First World War, stifled a sob.

"*Vey iz mir*, it's happening all over again," she said, not for the first time that week. "I never thought I'd live to see such a war happen again. They told us that was the war to end all wars."

"Shhh, Mama," my mother replied. "Don't scare the children. This is nothing like that."

When our street was quiet again a few hours later, we stepped out of the basement, one by one. It was still daylight. We found a town that, on the surface, didn't look much different, apart from a few German officers here and there. But looks can be deceiving. In truth, everything in our world had changed.

Chapter 4

What Was the Beginning of the German Occupation Like for You?

Against the gray September sky, our beautiful *shul* looked like a building site, with exposed beams and walls standing off-kilter. If you didn't know better, you would think it was in the condition it had been in just fifteen years earlier: under construction. But this was the opposite. In fact, it was like watching a movie in reverse. Instead of putting up lumber, they were dismantling it. Instead of furnishings being brought in, they were being carried away. Even the Rabbi walked off with some of the sacred Torah scrolls, in order to keep them safe in his home.

Papa waved to a neighbor as he walked past our house, carrying a chair from the *bimah.*

"So you men are tearing down our synagogue," he said quietly, when he spotted the man, who was trying, despite the heavy load, to hurry by. He paused, grudgingly, and spoke without quite meeting my father's gaze.

"It's the Germans," he blurted, setting down the chair. "You know they plan to burn it down, but we couldn't take the chance. One strong gust of wind in the wrong direction, and all our houses would burn." He spoke with one hand on the back of the chair, as if afraid my father would snatch it from him. "Yours could, too, you know. So we offered to tear it down ourselves. To save the town, you understand."

My father nodded, his face grim. "So what are you doing with the lumber?" After all, he was in the business. His father had probably supplied it to the community to build the synagogue in the first place.

The man shrugged. "What do you think? We're keeping it. After all, we're doing all the work." And with that, he went on his way, struggling with the unwieldy furniture.

My father couldn't really blame them. In truth, we were sort of all in this together at that point. Not only had many Poles—considered "slaves of the Greater German Empire"—been taken for forced labor, but the Germans also commandeered their crops and animals with little thought of payment. They also took over the sugar factory, installing their own administrators in the factory villa. And a German police unit of twelve officers was stationed in one of the office buildings.

The German occupation of our town had started slowly, like a cancer. On the Friday after the invasion, once my father got word that he could return to town without fear of arrest, he made his way back. When he walked through the door a few hours before Shabbos, we greeted him like he was the Messiah.

"What did I miss while I was gone?" he asked, after the hugs and handshakes subsided.

My uncle shrugged. "Not much." He sipped his tea. "The Germans pulled together some of us to bury the dead Polish soldiers and horses. Disgusting work. Along with anything else they didn't want to do themselves."

I thought about this. A few days ago, it would have been unimaginable to have anyone force Jewish men to bury dead Polish soldiers. Now, no one batted an eye, except for my grandmother, who overnight had started to look even older than her ninety-three years.

"Did everyone get home safe?" my mother asked. "What about the Saltzman boys?"

"They kept heading east with some of the others. They think it's better being in the Russian zone. Who knows? Maybe they're right."

No one said anything. We had no idea what was the right course in this upside-down world.

All over town, refugees poured in from places that had it far worse. In many cases they were exhausted, hungry and scared. Our house was soon overcrowded. My father's sister Frymet had left her husband and their chocolate factory in Warsaw to come stay with us after the Germans arrived there. The Wolnermans, my mother's sister Ita and her husband Pinchas, joined us, after seeing off their grown sons, Adam and Moniek, to Russia. Much as we loved our family, all those people in one little house was a tight fit, especially when you had to step over snoring bodies on the floor to answer the call of nature in the middle of the night.

Early one evening not long after the Germans arrived, my little brother was walking out the door when my mother called him back.

"Where do you think you're going?" she asked.

He named a friend some distance away, saying he was going to work on a class project.

"Yulik, the whole town is under curfew. You can't leave the house after six. And besides, you know you're not allowed to go to school anymore. Stay where you are."

He looked at her in surprise. "They've closed the schools for good?"

"Just for Jews," I told him. "The *goyim* can go. They goyim can also leave town, but not us. C'mon. We can play marbles, if you want."

"Quietly," Mama cautioned, indicating one of the few beds in the house. "Your *bubbe* is trying to rest."

As bad as things were getting in our town, I was heartbroken when we heard about the fate of my beloved Krakow. The country was now divided, with the west going to the Third Reich, while the General Government, a separate administrative region known as Distrikt Krakow, was under the governorship of the German Hans Frank, based at the Wawel Castle. The plan for Krakow itself was to totally Germanize the city by removing some of the Jews and renaming everything in German. They even set about rewriting history in the newspapers, all in an effort to make it appear to have always been a German town.

One day during that strange period, I came home to my mother, seated in the front room in a rare display of tears.

"What is it, Mama?" I asked, running toward her.

"It's Wolf Dula. He was drafted with some of your other cousins, and now he's dead. And him the eldest son of that family. Killed like a dog by those Germans in Warsaw. Our capital. It's a *shondeh*."

Still our immediate family was lucky. Most Jewish businesses were taken away, either given to Polish refugees from the west or, if they were profitable enough, to Germans, often along with the owners' homes. But not ours. Not yet. As always, we were privileged. We were able to bribe the German police and administration. Yet my parents knew that luck can run out at any moment. One day, my father decided to sit down at the lumberyard with his Polish partner Wojiech Guca.

"I think you should take over the business," he said. "Otherwise the Germans will steal it away from under our noses."

Guca readily agreed. Why wouldn't he? "What about the land?" he suddenly asked. The previous year, he and his brother-in-law Thomasik had gone in with my father on a partnership for the ownership of several acres of timber outside of town.

My father frowned. This couldn't have been easy for him, after all he and his father had put into the business.

"I'll sign it over to you, as long as I can keep doing business with you." Papers were signed, and who knows what arrangements were made. They sealed the deal with a drink, although to my father, the vodka must have tasted especially bitter. But at least the lumberyard and the land were safe, even if they were no longer ours.

Because many of the Poles were sent to Germany to work the farms and other jobs that the soldiers couldn't do, the Judenrat, the newly formed local governing council of the Jews, was ordered to choose fifteen people to be employed as slave labor in the sugar factory. The Germans set up the system of Judenrats to decide the fate of their brethren when it came to taxes, registration and forced labor, money collection and food rationing. Because of my father's prominence, not to mention his ownership of a telephone, our Judenrat, composed of three local *macher*s—the businessmen Michal Spkokoiny and Itzche Aspis and the tailor Zelek Fischler—from the local *k'hilah*, the existing Jewish council based in the neighboring town of Kosycze, met in our home. My father, although not a member, served as the unofficial secretary. As a former high school student, I helped with the books. There were times when we could bribe the Germans for something we needed with new boots or clothing, but when they had their orders, we couldn't ignore them. The town now also had our own Jewish police, who wore special yellow hats in the small towns, but got real uniforms in the cities.

Sometimes it seemed as though everyone in town worked for the Reich now. The Jewish tailor on our street was ordered to make uniforms for the administrators. Many others did manual labor like street-cleaning or snow removal. I was able to get by doing odds jobs in our lumberyard, which was still considered necessary for the war effort. Later on I too worked in the German administration, cleaning the garage and maintaining their two cars.

It was a quiet fall night when Papa gathered us all together to pass out white armbands with blue Stars of David. We looked at them in surprise.

"What's this?" Aunt Frymet asked him. "Wait, are these like the ones in Wloclawek?" We had just read that Jews in that town had been wearing something similar.

Papa frowned. "The same thing."

"How are we supposed to put it on?"

"Like so." Papa slipped the armband over the right sleeve of his shirt till it rested around his upper arm. "It's got to show at all times when we're outside, so when it's cold, we would put it on the coat."

"Does Yulik have to wear one?" I wondered. "After all, he's just a kid."

"That's what they say. Anyone over age ten."

"What happens if he doesn't?"

My father shook his head. "You don't want to know, Shmuel. Just do it." Here he turned to the rest of the family. "All of you."

Day after day, the situation got worse. In the winter, they wouldn't let people keep their fur coats. One woman my mother knew was shot point-blank because she refused to give up her mink to the Germans. My father told me that story after the others had gone to bed. I guess he thought I was a man now. Then he said, "You know, I heard that one of the younger German policemen who came into Molenda's bar the other night got very drunk. He was talking to some of the men about something or other. Sounding off. Then all of the sudden he cried out, 'Adolf Hitler is a bastard!'"

"Supposedly nobody really thought much of it at the time," he went on, "but his friends were quick to get him home to sleep it off. Somehow, even to that German, it was as if none of this is real. I'm hoping this will all blow over soon, son. This is Poland, after all." I nodded.

What we didn't realize, what we couldn't know, was just how wrong we were. This wasn't Poland. Not anymore. This was the Third Reich.

Chapter 5

What Made Your Family Go into Hiding?

"Oh bubbe, oh bubbe!"

It was just about the only thing anyone in the family could think of to say, other than "We love you," and "We are so so sorry."

My ninety-three-year-old grandmother Perel sat keening—there is no other word for it, really—at the table, my parents' faces were red and creased with heartbreak, and Papa's sister kept shaking her head and leaning over to pat or hug her mother. Only the two younger boys, my cousin Shmuel and my brother Yulik, seemed too stunned to express their sorrow.

As for me, I could not believe this was happening. We were about to go into hiding without my grandmother. Because she was too old and weak to walk, not to mention live in squalor, she would be left here to meet the Germans on her own.

"What if I carried her on my shoulders?" I pleaded. "Or we could take turns!"

Everyone, including Bubbe, looked at me like I was crazy.

"It's six miles away," my father said somberly. "And if anyone saw you doing that, or any of us, they would know immediately what was going on. We would all be at risk."

"We just don't know what we're going to come up against, Shmulik," my uncle said, shaking his head. "Either on the way or when we get there. She's very frail. It would be cruel to put her through that."

"But we can't just leave her here!" I cried. "That's even crueler! What will happen to her?" As soon as I asked the question, I regretted uttering it out loud.

There was a stony silence, except for the now muffled sound of my grandmother's weeping. At last she raised her head to speak.

"Be good to each other," she said. "Don't worry about me. I am old already. I have lived a long life. Just lead good lives and be good to each other. And don't forget me."

I ran to her side. "We will come back, Bubbe!" I said. Even as I spoke the words, I knew very well that they were meaningless. We might get back someday, but she would be long gone by then.

The unimaginable had happened, and it had happened not only to us. All around town, we knew people were dealing with their own versions of horrendous loss. One by one we kissed her and took her blessing, and then we slipped out of the house and into the night.

We hadn't planned to go into hiding in the late summer of 1942. Everything leading up to it happened slowly and methodically. If you had left the country for a few months, you wouldn't believe the changes on your return, But living there day after day was like drips from a poisoned faucet, one by one.

Our house had been a hub of activity. Not only our Judenrat, but those from surrounding towns met in our living room to do business with the local German authorities. My mother was always serving tea and *mandelbrot* to prominent men from Koszyce, Dzialoszyce, or Skalbmierz. My father let me sit in when appropriate, sometimes to take notes.

At first, we were still getting word about the outside world from our big, cabinet-sized radio, or from the town's two Jewish newspapers. But after a while, the only sources of information available to us were the German authorities, the visiting Judenrat members, the odd refugee from the cities, or each other.

In June 1941, we learned that Germany attacked the Soviet Union. They soon executed one million Jews throughout areas our people had inhabited for centuries: eastern Poland, Hungary, Ukraine, Belarus, Lithuania. They expanded their string of labor camps for developing munitions. Then, in January of the following year, the Nazi leadership held the Wannsee conference at a villa in a beautiful lake district in southwest Berlin. Its goal: to determine the Final Solution to the "Jewish Question," which they determined was the establishment of concentration camps throughout Europe, equipped with gas chambers to carry out the ultimate in modern, efficient mass extermination. Of course we didn't know that part at the time. If we had, there would have been mass panic in the streets.

Meanwhile, the Nazis had already set up ghettoes in the major cities, including of course Warsaw and Krakow. They were not only penning in the people who had previously lived freely there, but deporting others to the ghettoes from outside. My father and uncle often debated what would be better, going to a ghetto or being free. On one hand, a ghetto was by definition located where people were already living, where there was civilization, infrastructure, where goods and services were still available, if rationed. On the other, you were stuck there, either permanently or at least for the hours of curfew. And the Germans could monitor your movements. If they wanted no schools, no prayer, no gatherings, they could easily punish those who disobeyed their orders.

"At least if we get to a ghetto sooner rather than later, we might have a better shot at staying together, and at getting better accommodations," my uncle suggested.

"Ha! They're already crowded there like rats," my father hissed. "And from what I hear, they're sick and starving. Soon they'll all be sent God knows where. But at least the Americans have entered the war. Let's hope this will all be over before we have to set foot in a ghetto, or anywhere else."

"What do you mean, God knows where?" my mother wailed. "You think if God knew the rumors we hear about what they're doing to the Jews, that He would stand for it?" No one acknowledged the remark. Not that we were a religious family. During Yom Kippur services, I used to pull out cookies to enjoy at breaks from the football game in the shul parking lot.

"Maybe they'll just forget about us?" I chimed in. I was desperate to find a light among the darkness that surrounded us.

Papa clapped me on the shoulder. "Sure, sure," he said lightly. "Or maybe they'll just decide that our little town isn't worth the trouble." He tried to chuckle, but the sound came out more like he was choking. "Anyway, I say we go into hiding. Mleko said we can all stay with him." We all knew Mleko. He was the *soltys*, or head of the township. It was good to have such powerful friends.

"Where does he live?" Aunt Frymet asked. We were talking so quietly and intently that we hadn't noticed that she'd entered the room. My aunt already knew there would be no room for her in the barn; my father had arranged another hiding spot for her.

"About six miles from here. We can walk it easily."

"And Bubbe? How will she manage?"

For several minutes, it seemed, no one dared breathe. Then my father said, "Look, this is just a precaution. As I say, it may all be over before we need to go."

We learned that they were starting to empty the ghettoes in the big cities, followed by the smaller towns not far from ours. They were shooting the elderly and sick by the hundreds. In Dzialoszyce, which before the war had boasted 10,000 Jews, we heard there was a mass grave that may have held as many as a thousand of our people.

Then, that summer, a spate of new rumors filled our ears like gnats. My friend Fischler told me that one of the German administrators told a tailor who was making clothes for him that something big was happening Monday.

Our friends in the Polish police told us that the Germans had ordered extra transit for Monday. One night, the driver I was working for at the garage invited me to dinner at his house. Over a meal of fried fish, he said there was an "action" about to happen, and he offered to let me hide with him. I thanked him and declined the offer without another word.

When we heard these things, everyone else did, too. All around us, people began to make plans to run. My father dug up the valuables he had hidden all those months before and left them for safekeeping with his friend and former brother-in-arms, the Polish nobleman who lived on the nearby estate. We began to prepare clothing and bedding to take to Mleko. All the time, we were careful not to say a word to anyone else. Even Jews, we knew, were working for the Gestapo, the Nazi secret police.

One evening over supper, Papa turned to my eleven-year-old cousin Masha.

"I've discussed it with your father," he said. 'There is a place waiting for you with the nobleman, at his estate not far from Bosczynek. It's not far; we can walk it in less than two hours. Your papa explained it to you, yes?"

She nodded. In a small, quavering voice, she said, "Papa said no one will know I'm Jewish, like they do with the men." She reddened a bit; everyone knew she was talking about circumcision. That's how they could spot a Jewish male in an instant, by making him open his pants.

Now Masha's voice and eyes filled with tears.

"But I don't want to go!" she wailed to her father, who was sitting across the table.

"We know," my uncle murmured. "No one wants you to. But it's for the best."

Her face, which had been red, suddenly grew icy pale. "What if the Germans come?"

"Your protector is a nobleman." Papa coughed. "They wouldn't dare bother him."

"Of course they won't," my uncle said quickly. "You will be very safe, there at the estate. We don't know what will happen in the future, but we're hoping we won't be separated for too long." When she didn't look convinced, he continued, "Look, your Aunt Frymet is with Mayor Prkop. The Woldermans from Lodz and Mina and Malka are at the Kocerbas in town. The Dulas are in hiding too, but we don't know where. We're all just doing what we can to survive, and you have to, as well."

Masha nodded, and that evening, after heartfelt good-byes, my father walked her over to the home of his powerful friend. Masha's mother, Aunt Leonka, never left her bed.

Since the invasion, the town elders had hoped that if we just did what the Germans asked, they would leave us alone. Unlike in the cities, the authorities had less control over us here in a small town. Then, at 7 a.m. one Monday morning in late August of 1942, we got the message over bullhorns in the streets that the following Monday we would all have to show up at a certain field at the edge of town. We were allowed to carry with us just one bag of belongings each.

"This is it," my father said grimly.

After midnight that Saturday, my father and I took off down the back roads to start preparing our family's hiding place with Mleko. Walking alongside him in the cool, sweet-smelling breeze, the quiet broken only by the barking of dogs as we passed, I felt a mixture of pride and terror. Pride that my father was entrusting me with this crucial duty. Terrified that it was necessary in the first place.

"Listen," said Mleko, as we sat in his front room some time before dawn, sipping tea. "I've been thinking. It's too dangerous for your family here." My heart sank, but my father said nothing. "Because of my job, there's a holding cell here in the house, which means there's more activity, and the Germans have more reason to sniff around. It's too dangerous." He puffed on his pipe. "But don't worry. I've got something else for you that's much safer."

He led us to the nearby home of his brother-in-law, a poor farmer.

What was there to say? Five more from our household joined us in Boszczynek the next evening, and our new life began. We had to remind ourselves that we were very lucky to have it.

Chapter 6

How Did It Feel to Be in Hiding?

I was lying on my back in a narrow hole in the dirt floor of the grain barn, looking up at the slatted ceiling through gaps in the wooden plank above me. My father and uncle had dug seven of these holes weeks earlier, each about six feet deep. Maybe it was a coincidence, but they were just the right size for coffins.

The barn was airless even in better times, and now it stank with the odor of the bucket in the corner that we used for an outhouse, mixed with the mentholated tang of my father's ever-present Ben-Gay for his aches and pains. Buried in the earth with the plank over my head, I could barely breathe. I was terrified, but at least it was a change from the boredom of the last few days.

All I could think was: How long will we have to go through this? And then: What will happen when we finally have to leave? Is it going to be better or worse?

And then, just when I'd imagined things couldn't get much worse, shots rang out in the distance. One. Two. Three. Four. Five. Six. I lost count after ten or twelve.

My family lay in their holes all around me, within whispering distance. We knew that our loved ones and friends could have just been murdered. But no one dared make a sound.

We didn't always lie there in the holes, only in times of extreme danger, when, for instance, an outsider got too close. The plan was for us to sit in the dark barn by day, in a sort of walled-off area in the middle. We could walk outside for a few hours every evening to get a little air and exercise or, later into the fall, to go into the poor farmer's primitive house from time to time to warm ourselves. Mleko's brother-in-law was a kind man, and every night he sent his hunchbacked son to feed us bread, cheese, or a bit of fruit, maybe occasionally some hot food as well, such as the occasional potato or scrap of meat. He had to be always on his guard, because if anyone caught on that he was feeding Jews, he—and we—would surely be killed. Looking back, he must have been as scared as we were, but at the time, all I could feel was envy that just because he wasn't a Jew, he was free to step out into the sunshine. To live his life. My own life seemed so far away, already a vanishing dream.

After the shootings, we were anxious to hear what the farmer's son could tell us. On occasion he brought a Polish paper for us to read, but mainly, he was our primary source of information. That night, when the young man had settled the bundles of food on the floor, we sat not far from him, waiting for the women to apportion it. I could see from my father's tense shoulders that he could not stay silent much longer. He knew the boy would want to leave as soon as he could.

"What was the shooting we heard today, son?" he asked at last. Since being forced to give up his heavy cigarette habit, my father was often testy. Not that the impossible situation didn't prey on all our nerves.

The boy swallowed hard. "The Germans put out the word that anyone who returned to town would be okay," he began. "So many of the Jews came out of hiding."

"We know," my uncle said. "You told us that last week."

"Well they put them all in a school, you know, and then t-t-today—" The simple boy was at a loss for words, and I couldn't blame him. It was the first time I realized how young he was. He was as unprepared for this as my cousins and I were. I looked over at my little brother. He had always been quiet, but at that moment I couldn't recall the last time I had heard his voice.

"What?" Papa asked the farmer's son, as gently as he could manage. "Tell us, please. How many did they execute? Do you have any idea?"

He spoke so quietly we could barely hear him. "I think about 300."

"What did he say?" my mother asked my father from a few yards away.

"Three hundred," he hissed at her. Then he turned back to the farmer's son.

"Do you know—do you know any of their names, by any chance? Even one or two?" The boy shook his head fiercely and, before my father could say another word, he disappeared into the darkness.

The next day we learned more. My mother's sister Ida Wolderman and her family, who had been hiding in a neighboring village with about a dozen others, were among the dead. To say my mother was inconsolable is to put a word on emotions that can't be named. I had never seen her so broken. Up to that point, Mama had always joined in the general whispered conversations we engaged in to break the miserable monotony of our long, dark days. But it wasn't until several weeks after hearing that her sister was shot that she showed any signs of wanting to remain among the living.

My father would go every once in a while in the dead of night to check on Masha. Nobody liked that he did it, my mother least of all. But to be fair, he argued, it was he who had made the arrangement with the nobleman, and he felt responsible for her safety. The rest of us waited on tenterhooks till he returned with the news that she was alive. It was funny, really: She was in point of fact so much safer than we were, with the nobleman in the house to protect her.

One night several weeks after we went into hiding, Papa was gone on his visit to Masha for much longer than usual, and my mother was quietly hysterical. I say quietly because the whole time we were there, no one ever actually cried or shouted. We suffered our agony without making a peep.

"She's our daughter," my aunt murmured to her husband. "You should have gone yourself."

"Don't you think I offered?" he replied between gritted teeth. "But your brother wouldn't hear of it. You know him. He's very strong-willed. And capable. I'm sure he'll be fine. They both will be fine. You'll see."

My mother gave him a strange look, as if she were seeing not him, but my father, in her mind's eye, so many miles away. "You'll see," she repeated dully. "They'll both be fine."

Just then the barn door opened a few inches, and in slid a familiar figure. It was my father, for some reason I couldn't fathom looking like he was laden with bundles. We all breathed a sigh of relief until another, smaller figure entered, wearing what appeared to be a backpack. It was impossible to see much of anything in the dim light of the barn, and of course my father never went out when the moon was full.

"Mama, Papa, it's me!" Masha whispered, taking an uncertain step forward. "I'm here with you at last!"

No one spoke right away. Was this good news? We couldn't tell.

Then my father said, "Masha was so unhappy with the nobleman. She begged me to take her here to be with the family. I couldn't say no."

"He didn't hurt me," my cousin added quickly. "I just couldn't stand to be away from you. Not to know what was going on. If you were okay. Please don't be mad at me! I came back because I love you. I was so lonely and scared."

I knew them all so well; it was as though I could hear everyone's thoughts. Now we have eight mouths to feed. Eight people to worry about. Another hole to dig.

There was Papa, Mama, Yulik and I, my mother's brother Yasef and his wife Leonka, who was also my mother's sister, their son Shmuel, and now, once again, their daughter Masha.

On the other hand, at the most terrible time in our lives, we were together. That had to be a good thing, right?

Chapter 7

What Was Happening in Your Town While You Were in Hiding?

"All right, I'll tell you. I'll tell you everything my father has told me, everything I heard or saw for myself. Then you've got to leave me alone about it."

Each night we waited eagerly for the farmer's son, not only for him to feed us, but, equally importantly, to hear news of Kazimierza Wielka. It took some time till we were told the details of the liquidation of the Jews of our town, however. What changed we couldn't know; maybe our host just finally took pity on us, realizing that ignorance can be less blissful than closure. Or maybe he'd finally had enough of our pleading.

Until we went into hiding, all we knew after three years of German occupation had dwindled into rumors about what was happening to people, rumors that swirled through our town like the odor of bad fish. But at least we could look around for ourselves, trust our senses and get a variety of opinions and perspectives, sometimes from Polish authorities, occasionally from our occupiers themselves. We knew that the Germans kept winning battles in the East, that few of the towns and cities in Poland had any Jews left in them. *Judenrein*, that's what the Germans called it. Free of Jews.

But where had they all gone? Nobody knew for sure, and if they did, they weren't saying. Had they vanished to ghettoes in Warsaw, Krakow, or elsewhere? To the homes and farms of kind neighbors? Or were they simply dead? This was no idle intellectual exercise. For one thing, we had dozen of relatives in town, on both my mother's and father's sides. For another, we worried about our own eventual fate.

And so he told his story.

"It was the fourth of September," he said slowly, suddenly fascinated with a hangnail on his right thumb. We were circled around him in various positions on the barn floor, lying on blankets or sitting bolt upright or standing against the wall that divided our hiding place from the rest of the barn.

"That much we know," my uncle said. "Three years to the day since they arrived. The Germans are nothing if not organized." When his wife quickly shushed him, we all understood. We didn't want to spook the boy. We needed to hear this. Every word.

"The fourth of September was a Sunday, you remember. Everywhere were soldiers with bullhorns driving through the streets, yelling out the newest rules. At 7 a.m. the next morning, every Jew had to get to the field by the rynek. They were allowed to pack a few things to take with them." The rynek was the market area, known also as the *stawisko*. Mondays were market day. It was as though on that Monday, the Jews were the products instead of the shoppers.

He paused, long enough that we knew someone would have to ask the question. Our eyes met; at last seven pairs of them settled on Papa. And so my father asked, "And what happened to the weak or elderly, the ones who couldn't come?"

"What do you think?" The young man spat out the words. When no one answered, he took the silence as an invitation to elaborate, although at that moment, I'm not sure anyone wanted him to. "They ordered the Judenrat and Jewish police to help them round everyone up who was moving too slowly. Then the Germans themselves searched the houses for anyone who hadn't made it out. Some of the older people they shot."

Papa swallowed, just once. "And my mother? Do you by any chance know what happened to her?" He had asked before, of course, many times, but he had never gotten a straight answer.

This time, the boy didn't blink. It was as if he forced himself to lock eyes with my father, to be man enough to tell him to his face.

"My uncle made a point to check. They shot her. Right in front of your house."

The silence that followed felt like it would last the rest of our lives, like none of us would ever speak again, like there would never be anything else to say. Never a song, never a story or a joke would pass among us, and never, ever a prayer. If no one filled this silence fast, I thought, it would last till the end of time.

When he managed to speak again, my father's voice was flat and quiet, as if all the air had been pumped out of him.

"And the bodies of the murdered? What happened to them?"

The boy shrugged. "They said that Mandecki and . . . Spokoiny?"

"Yes, Spokoiny," my uncle said. "From the Judenrat."

"Well, I heard they and some of the others collected the bodies. They took them on Spokoiny's wagon and buried them. Outside the Polish cemetery, I think." Before anyone had a chance to ask he added, "At least a dozen corpses. I mean bodies. I mean people."

It was all the younger kids could take in for the night, and they drifted outside with my aunt to mourn in peace. Only Papa, Mama, my uncle and I remained.

My father whispered, "What else?"

"Umm, I heard stories about people you told me to ask about. I don't know how many of them are exactly true." At every pause the adults grew restless; I could see them forcing themselves to let him take his time.

"Your family, the Wolnermans?"

"From Lodz. They were hiding with Mina and her daughter Malka."

"Well, I heard that they were shot; I don't know if it was by the Polish or the German police. They were on their way to Slomniki." Slomniki was maybe twenty miles from where we were hiding, in Bosczynek. I felt a shiver go through the four of us.

"And the butcher's daughter. She was shot in the street. Another girl, I think her name was Tchasnik, same thing. And the Kozuch family. They took their time getting from the house that Monday morning. The Germans were waiting for them, sitting on the front steps. Four Germans and two Polish police, they say." He shook his head. "The policemen were drinking vodka, and they asked the neighbor, Mrs. Kita, for some glasses. Then when the Jewish Kozuch family came out with their bundles, they shot at them. The two adults were dead. The boy they missed, and he managed to run to the group." He considered. "Could be dead by now anyway."

We hated to hear more, but at the same time we were hungry for it.

"On Glowackiego Street, there was an old woman; she had missed the 7 a.m. deadline. As she got to the gate, this German with a cigarette dangling from his mouth fired two shots at her, and she was gone."

My mother had seemed as though she were barely paying attention, but now she looked up at the young man.

"What—do you know what happened to the homes? To our things?" We knew she didn't care nearly as much about these as she did the people. It was just easier to hear.

Young Mleko shrugged. "When the Germans got, um, rid of the Jews, the city officials sealed off their houses. I don't know, maybe for safekeeping. But right away people came and broke the seals. They just helped themselves to whatever they could carry: candlesticks, silver, furniture, anything. I guess the town fathers figure that if the valuables were going to be taken, they might as well make a profit off of them. They auctioned off the rest."

Mama turned away, as though she were sorry she'd asked. But by now our newsman was on a roll. It was as though once it was primed, he couldn't turn off the pump.

"And Spoikony, the Judenrat guy?" he continued. My father and uncle nodded. "He and the rest of the committee picked up a bunch of the people who were grouped together in the field and took them on wagons to the station. The plan was to put them on the *koleika* to Miechow, then switch to boxcars on the regular tracks." He picked again at his thumb. We waited, not daring to breathe. I was picturing the switch from the narrow tracks of the koleika.

"Well, he got there too late. The Germans are sticklers for time, they say. They shot them. Shot them all." He stood up. "Then there are the stories of Poles who hid Jews for a little while before deciding they didn't want them anymore and—"

At that my mother put up a hand. This newest piece of information was hitting way too close to home. "Enough! Thank you, that's enough for now." No one had the heart to disagree.

Years later, I heard more. How that same Spokoiny asked Max Mandecki to look after his wife and children, whom he'd hidden with some local Poles. In exchange, Max said, the Judenrat man had let him forget the debt he owed him for grain. But Mandecki admitted to me that he never did follow up, and Spokoiny's family perished.

Then again, there's a small piece of good news I learned later: One man managed to evade the shooting of the Jews kept in the school. Our relative Israel Levenstein slid down a rope out a window one night and ran off to the Krakow Ghetto, while the other Jews who had returned from hiding were shot in the forest of Slonowice. But his wife and child he had to leave behind.

I guess when you think about it, that wasn't such good news either. All in all, Jewish life ended in the small towns and villages of Poland in the fall of 1942. There is nothing, nothing at all, that's good about that. No matter how you look at it, that was a full-blown catastrophe.

Chapter 8

What Was It Like Getting to the Krakow Ghetto?

As much as I had hated living in that cramped, dirty, smelly old barn, leaving it for the last time after two months was one of the hardest things I've ever done. The barn, bad as it was, represented shelter and safety; it represented my family. Outside on the road—although it was a treat to breathe in the fresh, frigid air—was, quite simply, hell. Being outdoors, especially during the day, was for us little more than a game of Russian roulette. For the authorities and ordinary Poles, on the other hand, it was a blood sport. It seemed as though everyone was hunting for Jews like us, those who had gone into hiding. The Germans gave the Poles a pound of sugar as bounty for anyone they brought in, dead or alive.

The day my father and I left the barn was the culmination of weeks of debate, mainly between him and my uncle, as to what was the safest plan for us. The talk went around in circles: The barn was a known commodity. We were safe, and it was getting cold outside. But it was only a matter of time till someone found us out. Did we want to take that chance? But what if we got caught on the road?

"Mleko is a good man," my uncle pointed out. "We know he isn't doing this for profit. It's something he believes in, saving us. Sticking it to the Nazis. I'm sure he wouldn't give us up. Neither would his son."

My father shook his head. His face, which had become pale and gaunt like all of ours, was grim. "That's not the point. They might not have any choice. Staying here is putting them at risk, as well. What do you think will happen to them if the authorities find us here?"

Meanwhile, we were receiving regular reports from Uncle Isaac and Aunt Sarah Levenstein, who were by now living with their two brave children in the Krakow Ghetto. We knew Jews in the Ghetto were regularly deported and killed. We also knew that conditions were cramped at the Levenstein home; not only was their family there, but my uncle had also invited his business partner Hochermen to bring his wife and two daughters, so that meant eight people were already jammed into a two-bedroom house. Food was adequate, we knew, but sanitation was less than ideal, despite the families' best efforts. Our presence would only make things harder for everybody. But by then we were thinking we didn't have much choice. When it's a matter of life or death, small things like space are no longer important. Your attitude changes so fast you don't even realize it.

We had long ago given up any pretensions of grandeur. The old ways—nice clothing, good china, hot meals—they seemed like the remnants of another life. Like animals, all we cared about now was survival. My father, as the older brother, made the final decision, but everyone agreed. We would go.

So here we were, my father and me, as before, making up the advance party. We were masquerading as peasants out for a brisk, early morning journey. The nobleman's two horses drew us in his wagon, which was jammed with clothing and odds and ends we had brought from the barn. I can only speak for myself, but my heart was in my mouth the entire ride, and I'm sure my father wasn't much calmer during all those hours. Astonishingly, we weren't stopped once during the long journey. I'm not so sure I could have said a word, or stopped shaking, if we had been.

When we arrived in the section of the city known as Podgorze, we knew we had reached our destination. The Jews had been moved from the old Jewish quarter of Kazimierz, the place I knew and loved, to a neighborhood on the other side of the Visla River. We told the Polish driver to follow along the barrier fencing, which fortunately for us was not electrified, until we could identify a hole wide enough to sneak through. What had other people used this break in the fence for? I wondered. To smuggle themselves in, or to smuggle themselves out?

"Stay put for a while," my father told the man, when we jumped down beside a good-sized gap. "We're just going to take a look at the situation. We'll return for our things as soon as possible." The driver rubbed his hands in the cold air and grunted in response.

We were frankly shocked by what we saw—not so much by how much had changed, but by how little. Apart from the wire fence, Krakow appeared at first glance to be its glorious old self, although it was dirtier, and fewer people walked the streets. We could almost believe that the war was a bad dream.

Then we saw another strange thing: People were travelling freely to and from the Ghetto. True, as Jews we weren't allowed to be roaming around wherever we pleased. But since we were disguised as good Polish peasants, we could have gone through the front gate, no problem, no questions asked.

It didn't really matter; we had made it safely. We just felt a little foolish that we had thought we were so clever, sneaking ourselves in. Now, all we had to do was retrace our steps back to the hole in the fence and get our things.

But when we got there, the driver had already gone. My father looked right and left, cursed and stamped his feet and raged for about half a minute, and then it was over. After all, things were just things. And so we arrived at the Levensteins empty-handed.

"Glad to see you, peasants!" Uncle Isaac greeted us, still dressed as we were in our Polish costumes. From the kitchen, Aunt Sarah rushed to bring us each a hot drink. She handed me the cup with a special warm hug, and despite my age and all those people circled around, I had to fight back my tears.

"Sit, sit!" she said. "*Nu*, tell us, how was the trip?"

After waiting for this moment for so long, we found it curiously hard to talk. To be in Krakow with our extended family! To be drinking hot tea and eating mandelbrot at a nice, if crowded, table! It was a strange sensation, this normalcy, after living so long like animals.

At last my father managed to say, "We made it in one piece, that's all that matters. But the damned driver took off before we had a chance to get our things."

My aunt clicked her tongue. "You won't need much here, believe me. Anyway, where would you have put it? But we'll find you something for now." She hurried off, clearly relieved to have something to occupy her besides cooking and cleaning.

"The rest of the family will be here tomorrow," Papa went on. "The nobleman has been so helpful, lending us his wagon. Even if the driver is a thief!" He shook his head, but I could tell he wasn't angry anymore. As he had said many times, nothing mattered but that we were alive and together.

"Did you notice how quiet it is out on the streets?" my uncle asked. We frowned. We knew what was coming. "That's due to the selections. Actions. There are only a few thousand Jews left here now. And they've divided up the neighborhood into Ghetto A and Ghetto B. A is for the Jewish authorities and the able-bodied people who work outside, like us. The Jewish police chief, by the way, Shapiro, is a real son-of-a-bitch. You'll want to steer clear of him at all costs."

"What's Ghetto B?" I asked. In the old days I would have stayed quiet when adults were discussing serious matters, but with all the responsibility I was taking on, I was beginning to more forthright. Funny way to grow up, I guess, but that's what the times called for.

"That," Mr. Hochermen said quietly, "is for all those too old or ill to work. Or else those who can't find jobs."

"What happens to them?" I asked. No one looked at me, and no one answered, either. That told me all I needed to know.

"So," my father said, with a brightness I well knew he didn't feel. "Why did they move the Jewish quarter, anyway? Wouldn't it have been simpler to have just left everyone where they were?"

"You would've thought so," Uncle Isaac said. "The German governor, Frank, is holding court at the Wawel. He decided that was too close to the Jewish Quarter for comfort. Didn't want to be too near us Jews, you know. Didn't want to catch it from us!" His laugh, when it came, was hollow. "And yet, there are so many visits by the S.S. and the Gestapo, not to mention the German and Polish police, that you would think proximity would make their lives easier. Go figure!"

"These Germans are nothing if not smart and efficient," my father murmured. "I'm sure they have it all figured out."

We sipped our cooling tea in silence. I took another cookie. All we could hope for was that the other seven members of the family would arrive as safely as we did. Although when we looked around the dark, cluttered space, we couldn't imagine where we were going to put them.

Chapter 9

Can You Describe Life in the Ghetto?

Tired and hungry, I trudged through the streets from the Wachs metal factory toward one of the three gates into the Ghetto. From the outside, I could make out the bricked-up windows facing the city, the barbed wire encircling the buildings. But for them, and the fact that I was living in what was formerly a Polish neighborhood, I could have imagined it was four years earlier, and I was just a naïve schoolboy, away from home for the first time.

But it was February, 1943, the end of another workday, and war or no war, that means just about the same thing the world over: the need of a meal and a place to lay your head, to be yourself again for a few hours, with the people you love, who love you. In my case that meal was breakfast, because I worked the night shift.

If anyone had told me I'd grow up to be a machinist for the German army, I would have called them crazy. But Uncle Isaac had somehow finagled me the job. So here I was in the cold, early morning light, escorted from the factory by the Jewish police, checking in at the gates with the German and Polish police, then dragging my feet a few more blocks to Zgody Square, where my parents had been granted their own small apartment. From fourteen people jammed together, it was now just us. We knew how we were so fortunate to have found space. When a home was suddenly vacant, there was only one of two possible explanations. Deportation to the camps or execution. What the Germans called "actions."

Suddenly the trolley whizzed by me, slicing through the neighborhood on its electrified tracks. It never stopped, of course. Jews were expected to walk. More to the point, I think, no one wanted to share a trolley car with us. Suddenly Jews were strange and quite possibly poisonous in the eyes of people we'd walked by and done business with for centuries. *Verboten*, as the Germans said. Forbidden.

When I got to the house, my mother was ready with a relatively hearty breakfast. Food was rationed, but we didn't starve. For one thing, we could bring things in, like milk and bread, from the outside. A hot breakfast, and then my own bed. It was all I had to look forward to in the near future, and I didn't take it for granted. It was more than I'd had for quite some time.

When we first arrived in November, we quickly met others from our town: The Klausner family, Ptasnik, Wolf Aspis and his family, Wolk's sister Miriam, and Zekej Fischler with his son Avram. Uncle Isaac's brother Israel Levenstein was also there. He was something of a hero to us, having escaped the recent massacre in Slonowice. There were often get-togethers, at which people exchanged tidbits of gossip, like who from the Jewish communities was now living on Aryan papers as Poles, hunting their fellow Jews as informants for the Gestapo. People also talked about the underground operating mainly outside the Ghetto walls, a Zionist youth organization known as Akiba.

"What exactly are they saying Akiba did?" my brother asked. It was rare that he participated in family discussions, but this was news about people more or less our age. It brought the war closer to home.

"They attacked the coffee shop near the rynek," I told him. I was about eighteen at the time, glad to show off my superior knowledge. "Cyganeria. On Christmas, of all days."

"Did it do a lot of damage?"

"Killed some Germans. Pretty impressive, for kids."

"And?" my mother asked, calling out from her dishwashing at the kitchen sink. "What did they do to them?"

"I'm not sure." We found out later, though. They executed the teens and then, as further punishment, sent several hundred Jews from Ghetto B to be gassed at Auschwitz, including Wolf Ptasnik from our town, a good man we had known all our lives.

The conversation moved on. Some family members shared rumors about the newest demands and restrictions from the Germans. Others talked about what was happening on the battlefields. We were the blind advising the blind, in many cases, only getting bits and pieces of information when and where we could.

"Now that the Russians have pushed back Hitler," one of the cousins said after we heard of the German defeat in Stalingrad, "maybe we'll get a quick end to this madness. Maybe the Allies will get inspired."

"It could just as easily work the other way around," Uncle Isaac's brother said thoughtfully. "This was not a quick victory. The Germans have already showed just how tough they are." He was right. Instead of caving in, they stepped up their efforts to liquidate the Jews of Poland.

Some members of my family were unhappy with their jobs at the small workshops in the ghetto, sewing and doing some light manufacturing. Those who worked in Oskar Schindler's enamel factory, mainly women, complained about the furnaces and the sulfuric acid they worked with, But all in all, everyone was very grateful to be employed. Without work, there was no life.

As for me, working outside the Ghetto, going in and out, having extensive contacts beyond its walls, this was a big plus. Not that it was so terrible inside. What was terrible was the fact that we had to be there at all. Elsewhere the communities were cleared of their Jews; some factories put their workers in their own camps. It was unimaginable. For us, though, life, for a change, was more or less peaceful. Our days took on a certain pattern. There were times that the overwhelming emotion in our hearts was simple boredom. At that point, boredom was a blessing.

And then, in the blink of an eye, the calm was replaced with terror. On March 13, 1943, a Saturday morning, the loudspeakers blared the kind of unspeakable order that so many of us had avoided in our own little towns: Pack a bag. Assemble on the main square, according to place of work. Shots rang through the air. Where were they coming from, everyone wondered. A guard told us it was the hospital. According to Nazi logic, the patients weren't going to assemble, so they had to be executed.

Numb with shock, I grabbed a few things, along with everyone else. When we reached Zgody Square, I was so tense that I almost forgot to hug my parents and brother before making my way, quick as I could, to Uncle Isaac and the other Jewish employees of the Wachs metal factory. The odor of anxious bodies, the hysterical cries, the faces twisted in grief—these I will never forget. I bit my tongue and tasted blood, reminding me that what I was experiencing was no bad dream.

It wasn't long before the German authorities, punctual as always, gave the signal to march, and although we had no clear knowledge of where we were headed, we could hazard a guess. Plaszow, the closest detention camp, was just a mile and a half away, down Jerozelimska. Jerusalem Street.

Meanwhile, the air was alive with gunfire. Those who dared to look back saw small bodies thrown from upper stories in Ghetto B, and people by the hundreds shot in the square. The distant screams were nearly drowned out by the incessant *thwack* of bullets hurdling through metal chambers, in search of human targets.

Soon the camp was in sight. It was built, appropriately enough, on the remains of a Jewish cemetery. For however long, this was to be our new home. We hadn't taken much with us, but it didn't matter. They would gather the rest and bring it along later, they told us.

If we hadn't been so horrified by the events of the day, we might have laughed at the foolish lie.

Chapter 10

How Was Life for You at Plaszow?

Standing at attention among the others from my barracks, I shook so badly with terror that I wondered how it was that I remained upright. The hiding in the barn, the illegal travel, the deprivation of the Ghetto—nothing had prepared me for the scene playing out in front of me. There on the gallows stood a young man about my age being hanged for the so-called crime of singing the *Internationale*, the anthem of the anti-Fascists. Or so said the Ukrainian police officer who had reported him. And even more horrible, as if that weren't enough, was the fact that the Jewish police officer ordered to execute the boy was his own relative.

> Stand up, the damned of the earth!
> Stand up, the convicts of hunger!
> To overcome misery and shadow
> Slave crowd, stand up! Stand up!

On the walk to Plaszow from the Ghetto, I had been afraid of what I would find at the camp. Hunger. Overwork. Harsh living conditions. The sheer unknown of it all. But never had it occurred to me just how afraid I'd be. From the moment I opened my eyes in the morning, to the moment I closed them at night, I felt as though I had become one of the damned.

After several hours of walking from the Ghetto, we had arrived at the entrance to the forced labor camp of Plaszow. It was located just about thirty miles outside Krakow, but it might as well have been another country altogether. The Germans had set up long, low barracks for kitchens, latrines, workshops and sleeping quarters. Our bunks, three stacked wooden shelves that slept more than eighty men each, contained just some straw and thin blankets. The latrine was a stinking hole in the corner. For 250 men.

They came around to take our money and valuables, but somehow, I managed to hide some cash. I knew from my experience in the Ghetto that it would come in handy later on. After a time, the bloc elder, the barracks supervisor, brought in two guys to distribute utensils and serve us each a bowl of soup and two slices of bread. To our surprise it was real soup, swimming with bits of potato and other vegetables. Real bread. I have to admit, we ate okay. We also got to keep our own clothes, even our overcoats. On that first day, I could almost believe we weren't prisoners, just workers staying in substandard employee housing. Maybe I could deal with this after all. That first night I slept fitfully, but somehow, amidst the snores and groans and smells of hundreds of men, I managed to drift into unconsciousness. I dreamed, that night, of my father's mother.

We were abruptly awakened in the crisp, cold dawn for steaming hot coffee and roll call. Standing at attention for hours in the big open square, waiting to be counted, like sheep, I spotted Uncle Isaac. I knew my father was not far, in another group, as was Yulik. My mother was with the women, beyond some wire fencing. The Banachs, Joe and Lily and Masha, had also arrived with us. Much as I ached for them, it was a comfort knowing they were close by.

We heard some barking of orders, then some work assignments. When I discovered what I was to do, I thought at first I heard it wrong. We knew that as we were leaving the Ghetto the day before, the young, weak and infirm in Ghetto B, hundreds of people, were murdered. Now, I was among the group of men sent to bury the dead. The bodies arrived at the camp in horse-drawn buggies. The prisoners who arrived before us had already dug up the hard-packed earth of the gravesites to form an enormous pit, saving the stones to pave the streets of the camp. Our job was to carry the bodies from the buggies and line them up in the hole, packed together like so many sardines in a can, in order to save space.

My main fear, once I got over the horror of handling corpses, was that I would recognize someone, that I would be throwing a close friend, a beloved relative, a respected neighbor into that pit. The whole time I cringed in anticipation of such a discovery. It was a small mercy that I did not know a soul.

That night, I dreamed about those bodies.

Uncle Isaac had been in the group that had cleaned out the ghetto. Aunt Mina had stayed behind in Ghetto B, hiding there with Esther and Shmuel, somehow eluding the house-to-house searchers who would have murdered them, along with most of the other children, because only the Jewish police and Judenrat were allowed to bring along their families. With the help of a friendly Jewish policeman, my uncle managed to get Mina and their children to safety, even going so far as to smuggle out the two youngsters to the women's barracks in trunks.

For the first few months, I didn't have much to do. After the long roll calls, those who had been assigned jobs marched to work, returning around 5 a.m., after which they were free for the rest of the evening. Since I had not been assigned work yet, I spent my days wandering around the camp along with my barracks mates, speaking to my relatives when I could, trying to stay out of trouble, and most of all jumping at every gunshot, and there were many. The selections—waiting at attention to find out who would live and who would be sent to die—were the hardest, of course. I saw more than one person pinch his cheeks, trying to bring back healthy-looking color in order to be considered able to work. No work, no life. That was how it was.

To keep up the illusion that this was just an employment situation, perhaps, there were no guards in the camp. The SS, the elite paramilitary corps of the Nazi operation, manned the watchtowers, along with Ukrainian guards. Inside were the Jewish police, some crueler than others, all under the command of the Austrian-born SS officer Amon Goeth, the same man who had supervised the liquidation of the Ghetto.

After a few months, I started back on the night shift at Wachs, the industrial manufacturer I'd been working for when I lived in the Ghetto. Every night I'd march two miles with my group, under guard, then two miles back in the morning. My father was already working in the carpentry shop in the camp; my mother was making military uniforms at a textile factory in the city. As for Yulik, he worked for Oskar Schindler at the enamel factory, along with our cousin Masha.

Work wasn't too bad. I was put on a machine making parts for carbon lamps for the war effort. The first morning I met my Polish supervisor, I immediately felt that she was to be trusted. By then I was beginning to gain a sort of sixth sense for these things, I guess. I was almost like an animal, relying on instinct to stay alive. That's what we had been reduced to.

One day, this supervisor called me into her cubicle.

"Rakowski," she said, her brow knotted in concern. "You're looking hungry. Try some of this nice cake."

I didn't know what to say. She was much older than I, and my superior, not to mention that I was a prisoner. I didn't want to offend her, and in fact I *was* more than a little hungry. Besides, these were not times in which to refuse food.

"Thank you, Ma'am." I took the piece of cake from her handkerchief and held it uncertainly in my hands.

"Go on, eat it. I made it myself. It's nice and fresh."

Dutifully I bit into the cake. It was moist, but I was so ill at ease that nevertheless, it stuck in my throat.

She watched me eat, apparently waiting for a response.

"Very good," I said at last. Then I repeated, "Thank you, Ma'am."

"Sure. You're a good worker. You have to keep up your strength. Some time I'll bring you some potatoes. Maybe a little meat. You can cook where you are?"

I thought of the carpentry shop stove my father had mentioned.

"Yes. Sure. My father does."

She nodded in that way people in authority have of dismissing you without a word. So I turned and went back to my work.

Over the months, she also contacted people back home to get more food and money for us. This was dangerous, of course, but it was worth the risk. Strangest of all, she sometimes brought me work to do that was already mostly completed. Why was she so good to me? Maybe because I was able to pay her something from time to time. Maybe she did it for others, too. We never knew where our luck would come from; we just blessed it when it came.

I still had to attend roll calls, of course, and they got more and more terrible as time went on. People who tried to smuggle things into the camp, to escape or to bring Jews in who had nowhere else to go, prisoners from the nearby jail—most of them were made to strip, and all of them were executed at Plaszow, either by hanging or by shooting.

Most terrifying of all were the random shootings, when Goeth would see something he didn't like as he walked his two big, scary dogs around camp. Or maybe he was simply in a killing mood that day. We never knew what was on his mind; we stayed as far away as we could. We stayed even further from the dogs. They were known to engage in random executions that were even more horrible to contemplate than those of their human master.

Yes, we were terrified at Plaszow. We never knew when we opened our eyes each morning whether we'd live to see another. Still, day-to-day life was almost tolerable there. That is, until it wasn't.

> He who lives on man is a criminal;
> Our enemy is our master:
> This is the eternal watchword.

Never had the words to the *Internationale* been so meaningful to us.

Chapter 11

How Did You Get to Pionki?

The air crackled with the coming winter as my workmates and I marched back to Plaszow after work. I could already see my breath in the cold. I was reaching the end of my fourth year under the heel of the Germans. Would they ever be defeated? Would life ever return to normal? It was hard to imagine, hard to remember our sweet, simple, normal existence back home.

As soon as we arrived at camp, we were told to march with the rest of our group to an isolated stockade, surrounded by barbed wire. No one knew what was going on. It was clear that this was no ordinary selection, but that didn't mean it was any better, either.

By evening, more prisoners had arrived, and the following day, still more. On the third day, when we could hardly stand the wait, the Jewish police, known at the camps as firemen, told us to march to the train station. Once there, we were ordered at gunpoint to climb aboard cattle cars. We had heard about these train cars, the destination of which was usually a death camp. The doors slid shut behind us, one hundred prisoners per car, with a heavy clack. I thought for the hundredth time: How could Jews treat other Jews this way? On another car, I knew, were my mother and Aunt Mina. I wondered how they were dealing with all of this. My heart hurt at the thought.

If I had felt like an animal up till now, at that moment I felt like a trapped and terrorized human being.

Little by little, the camp had been changing. By the summer of 1943, most of us were no longer allowed to work. Only those employed by Oskar Schindler or the military were in the fortunate position of being deemed essential. For everyone else, Plaszow had devolved into a concentration camp, designed for humiliation and execution. Most of us were prisoners, nothing more. For the vast majority, all contact with the outside world was a distant memory. Again, I was lucky. Being young and able-bodied, I was still working in an Army compound outside the camp. But how long that would last, I had no way of knowing. I had no control over my life, only my death. It was easy to be killed at Plaszow, but living was a different matter altogether.

Prisoners were arriving all the time now, and the shootings and selections for the Auschwitz death camp were in high gear. The day my father told me that Uncle Yosef Banach had been taken away, I sat numbly on my bunk, staring into space. I knew he had boils all over his body. I also knew that in normal circumstances, a doctor could probably have cured them. But these circumstances were anything but normal. My uncle was being put to death for the high crime of being sick, and there was nothing any of us could say, no one to appeal to. It was so unimaginable that my mind simply shut down.

Food got scarcer, as Commandant Goeth started selling what was allotted to us on the black market. The firemen were no better. The most offensive and brutal among them, Chilewicz and Finkelstein, seemed happy to assist their Nazi boss, as did the Jewish staff in his office. One favorite punishment was sending people to dig in the camp quarry, where the poor wretches had to carry enormous rocks back and forth, for no apparent reason. Anyone who disobeyed was shot.

It was September, 1943, in Plaszow. It was hell on earth.

Only when they shut us into those cattle cars did I understand that things could still get worse. How to express the horror of such a ride, the gasping for breath, the jostling to reach the cracks in the walls for a taste of fresh air, the stench of excrement, the clawing fingers of hunger, the cries of abject terror, the roaring of the car against the tracks? Most terrible of all, however, was the not knowing. All we could surmise, from the direction of the train on the tracks, was that we were travelling north, which meant we were not en route to Auschwitz, the death camp. That was something, at least. We were still relatively young and strong. Maybe we had yet to wear out our value to the Nazis. Grasping at this small strand of hope, we finally slept, somehow leaning at odd, uncomfortable angles against the walls and each other. No one wanted to chance the filthy floor if they could help it. I tried not to think about my family, but I had to wonder: where were my father, or my brother, or Shmuel Banach?

The next day we arrived, miserable with hunger and thirst, at Pionki, a camp made up of old warehouses set in the forested area around the town of Radom. We had traveled nearly 125 miles. No one knew exactly what kind of place this was. Were we going to work, or were we going to be killed? Marching through the camp that first day, we noticed that again the Ukrainian guards stayed outside; our overlords were all SS men along with Jewish police, the latter of whom were supervised by a man named Mendel from Kielce, the next town over. We noticed too that the buildings were spread far apart from one another, due, we learned, to the fire hazard of placing a nitrogen-based alcohol refinery—for making gunpowder—in close proximity to a coal-based power station. These two enterprises were in support of the camp's huge munitions factory, one of the largest in the country.

As before, they ordered us to hand over our valuables, as if we had anything much left. All I owned was some money, a 500-zloty bill, and I wasn't about to give it up. Then they sent us to the showers.

This was no small thing. By then, we had heard rumors about the infamous gas showers at Auschwitz and other death camps, so many among us were trembling as we undressed and entered the room. Clasping the cash tightly in my hand, I stood under a showerhead. When cold water spurted out instead of gas, we all sighed with relief. Some among us said a little prayer.

Then, as if on cue, we all burst out singing the Hebrew song "Mayim, Mayim." *Mayim* means water, and the tune was written a few years earlier by a Polish Jew, celebrating the occasion of finding water after a years-long search through the desert in Eretz Yisrael. The words to it mean, "Joyfully you will draw water from the wells of deliverance."

Ushavtem mayim b'sason mimainei hayeshua
Ushavtem mayim b'sason mimainei hayeshua
Mayim, mayim, mayim, mayim
Hey mayim b'sason.

Does it seem strange to sing at a time like that? Not when you realize that you're not in a death camp. That you might just live to see another day. At a time like that, water from a showerhead is a thing to celebrate.

Feeling a little better, we got dressed and went to the warehouse that was to be our dormitory. Again, there were three shelves for beds, but this time they had to accommodate two or three hundred. Again, I climbed onto the top bunk. They gave us bread and soup, and for the time being, we considered ourselves relatively safe.

Despite the shower, Pionki was filthy, with no sanitation to speak of. That first day, we saw prisoners walking the camp who were bone-thin, demoralized, haphazardly clothed. We learned that some of them had been there quite a while, including the healthier, more privileged shoemakers and tailors who served the needs of the factory manager, the Gestapo, and the Jewish police.

If there was no Goeth with his dogs here, there was not much food or warmth, either, and we were soon hungry and cold. Luckily, on the second day in camp, I was among twenty or thirty new arrivals from Plaszow assigned the job of loading and unloading trainloads of coal into small wagons and pushing them to the power station. It was not such bad work if your aim was to stay warm in the brisk weather.

One of our supervisors was the chauffeur of the factory manager, a high-ranking officer in the Luftwaffe, the German air force, named Dr.

Brandt. This Brandt had a chauffeur, who, according to the rumors, had a Jewish wife, and treated us fairly. For one thing, he never shouted abuse. And a few days after I started, he was eating a sandwich near where I was working when I noticed that a big piece of it had dropped to the ground. I looked up at him, wondering if I should say something, when I found him giving me a meaningful look before turning away. In one fluid motion, I reached down, grabbed the food and stuffed it in my mouth. There was no point in dusting it off on my clothing; I was covered with coal dust. This game of feeding me with dropped food went on for quite a while. It may just have saved my life.

The Polish supervisor, on the other hand, was a nasty anti-Semite. I soon hit on a plan to get along with him and accumulate some extra food.

"What is it you want, filthy Jew?" he asked when I showed up at his desk after work.

"I was thinking," I said, "that possibly you might want to do some business with me."

"Business?" he sneered. "What kind of business do I want with a Jew?"

"Lumber business," I said slowly. "My family has lumber in the countryside. Our Polish partner is in charge now. He would be happy to make you rich if you'll help me out a little."

The sneer slowly melted, and the man shrugged. Then he put out a sooty hand. I took it in mine.

"Maybe we can do business after all," he said.

It was a huge help, but I didn't fool myself. I was always only a shadow's distance from death.

The work was back breaking, and the winter, especially with bodies and clothing that were worn thin, was harsh. We were lucky to have access to the powerhouse, which was warmer, and the alcohol, which was ninety proof. The Polish laborers weren't allowed near it, so we traded spirits with them for bread. Still, the warehouses where we slept were horribly cold. That winter we didn't know which bothered us more, being hungry, worked to the bone, freezing, or ridden with lice. I voted for freezing.

Then one day, a train appeared, and we went to open the cars as usual. Instead of coal, in one of them, we found clothing, probably from the prisoners who had perished at Treblinka, the nearby concentration camp. Scarcely believing our good fortune, we quickly put aside our squeamishness and took what we could. After all, the owners of these pants and shirts and sweaters and coats would never use them again. But we, at least for the time being, were still alive.

Chapter 12

How Did You Leave Pionki and Where Did You Go?

Some of us younger men from the barracks stood around talking about nothing. Griping, more like it. What else was there to do with our free time?

"I can't take much more of this," one guy said. This surprised us all; he was usually one of the more optimistic among us. "There's got to be a way out."

No one said a word for several minutes. Then another one muttered, "The other day they hanged a kid. Just for stealing booze from the refinery. Can you believe it?" We all nodded. This wasn't news. We had seen it with our own eyes.

"You know," murmured the tallest and strongest among us, "I've been thinking. There may be something." We had been leaning against a wall, looking out at the woods. Now we all turned to him expectantly.

"Think about it. Our building is really close to the fence. Down below these warehouses are old steam pipes. A ready-made tunnel, practically. Once we get down there."

The first guy drew in his breath sharply. "You really believe we'd make it?"

"They just hanged three people for trying to escape," the first guy said. Again we all nodded.

Nobody had anything to add, so I said, "Well, if you really think it'll work, I can get some tools from the factory. Shouldn't be that hard, if all six of us worked on it at night."

The big one shrugged. "Let's do it."

This was spring, 1944. Along with the first stirring birds and budding leaves came a more welcome sign of life: the rumor that the Russians were advancing on the Eastern Front. It didn't take more than that to make us feel better, physically as much as mentally. We found we could endure almost anything as long as we had a little hope. And with hope, came thoughts of escape. The Vistula River was just ten miles from the camp, and the locals knew the area well. There were times that it seemed as though everyone with half a desire to live was digging a tunnel. And a few of them actually made it out.

Then came summer, and our bodies truly warmed for the first time in many months. It wasn't just the rising temperature: we could hear the artillery fire across the river. As the cracks of gunfire grew louder, our anticipation grew along with it.

On one particularly hot, hazy day in July, someone mentioned how there seemed to be more guards around the fence. People started whispering the dreaded word: Auschwitz. Was this to be our end, when we had endured so much, and the Russians were so close?

When we got the order to dismantle the munitions machinery, we figured it was going to Germany. Crews of 300 prisoners at a time loaded the machinery onto waiting boxcars. One Saturday, I was lying in my bunk when the beefy hand of a Jewish foreman reached up to grab me. I was to help load the trains. How to describe the back-breaking, thankless work of hauling that equipment? Returning to the barracks after we finished for the day, I realized with a start that aside from the privileged prisoners and the police, only our crew of 300 was still in camp.

"It's like a ghost town," I said to the bloc elder. "Where did everybody go?" It was a rhetorical question, the kind you really, really don't want answered.

He shrugged. "Where do you think?"

I felt my whole body grow cold. That meant only one thing. The death camp.

"Meanwhile," he continued, "we've got some bodies to bury. Tomorrow we go back to work."

"Some bodies?"

"From the liquidation of the camp, idiot. You think it was easy? You think people had no idea where they were going?"

All I knew for sure was that my immediate family was not among them. Whether or not they had been killed earlier, however, I had no idea. Whenever my brain drifted toward them, I quickly pushed it in another direction. There was nothing I could do to help. And I wasn't raised to pray. I could only hope for the best. That included what everybody else in that group hoped: that we could avoid our probable fate. That when the job would be done, the Germans would be finished with us.

That's when we started making the plan to escape. It gave us renewed energy. Having a goal that was more than simply staying alive was a gift. Funny how sometimes that's all it takes. Digging around the pipes to enlarge the existing space was tiring work, not to mention dirty and dangerous, so we took turns. Most important of all, of course, was the fact that we had to keep the plan secret not only from the authorities, but also from the other men, who were not always to be trusted. Anyone, we knew, would do just about anything to curry favor with someone in charge in exchange for a shot at survival. Not that we could blame them. We just couldn't take any chances.

Two weeks of difficult, hazardous work we put into that tunnel, all after doing hard labor for the Germans. But then, when the fateful night came for escape, only four of us made the attempt. Another kid and I tried to explain to the others why at the last minute we decided not to go. Given how close the Russians were, I couldn't see taking the risk. The other guy just said he didn't feel right about it. So the four remaining escapees bid us farewell, and we wished them luck. Then they left us, to literally cover their tracks. When the fourth head disappeared down the hole, I felt a twinge of regret, but I had made my decision, and that was that.

Sometime later, I learned the fate of the escapees. Out of the four, two made it to safety. One of these was a close friend, Abraham Singer. Polish partisans shot the other two in the woods.

We knew from experience that the faster we worked, the sooner we might be executed. But the job had to come to an end, and one day it did. So when the Radom Gestapo chief came with Dr. Brandt to address us, we were surprised, but, as always, on our guard.

"You prisoners have one last duty to the Reich," Dr. Brandt said. "We know you will fulfill it well. You are going to the Fatherland to rebuild the factory there. It is an honor you do not deserve."

That night, the doors of the cattle cars slid shut behind us just as the Russian artillery fired yet again. How soon would our torment end? And how? Although we hadn't been quite as terrified as we were in Plaszow, our year in Pionki had at least been one more year of life. And yet we knew we were among the fortunate ones, if only because the Germans still needed us for a while longer

By now, we were more used to the unsettling experience of a dark, putrid cattle car. On the way south, we somehow managed to settle in. Some were snoring softly, when suddenly we were shaken by loud explosions and gunfire. The train abruptly stopped. I looked around, and more than one of the men was bleeding.

We were outside of Kielce, it turned out, when the Polish partisans attacked us, thinking the train was an army transport. The tracks were a mess, the engine had derailed, and work crews were sent to repair the damage. We were stuck for the rest of the day.

From out of the darkness, a deep voice asked, "Why don't they let us help?"

"And risk an escape? Never."

"Too bad the partisans didn't think to save us, while they were here."

"At least they managed not to kill us. That would have been something, huh?"

"The hell of it is, there's nothing we can do, locked in here in the dark."

Everyone agreed with that. It was unbearably depressing.

The following day, we arrived at a small Polish village called Mawsy Wielkie. It was to be our temporary home. It seemed the Germans had still more plans for us.

Chapter 13

What Was It Like Getting to Sachsenhausen?

I really can't go any further with my story without making it clear that since we were together at Pionki, I hadn't the slightest idea where my parents and brother were, or whether they or any other family members were even still alive. I don't imagine that too many people would have any problem imagining how hard this was for me, but just in case, let me explain.

Until I got to Pionki, I had lived every single day of the nearly twenty years of my life in constant contact with my family, and the first fifteen surrounded by literally dozens of relatives in the town where we had lived for generations. My family was my foundation, my mainstay, my identity. Even when I went to Krakow to high school, I stayed with my aunt and uncle and cousins. And even in that first camp, Plaszow, I could see my parents and brother. Now, I was completely alone in the world.

Today, children go to boarding school or sleep-away camp all the time; teenagers leave home for college. In the vast majority of cases, they are there by choice, treated well, and able to contact their parents, whether in case of emergency, or just to chat. There is generally not a war raging; they are not in constant fear of punishment or death. They have a pretty good idea that they will see their parents again. And even then, many of them experience isolation, if not sheer wretchedness.

Throughout that terrible time, I needed every shred of my wits and strength of character to survive with no knowledge of my family. I also needed hope. I had no faith to speak of, so I had no one to pray to. I had only myself to rely on, and the few friends I believed I could count on.

For the time being, at least, that would have to be enough.

Poland is beautiful in late July. It can get pretty warm, but once you've lived through the crystal-cold winters, the heat is a welcome respite. And when you're outside in the country at night, the stars put on a spectacular show.

It was toward the end of one such shimmering day in July, 1944, when soldiers pulled us out of the boxcars and directed us to a large barn. There were several hundred of us there to feed and house, but the Germans had thought of everything. Within a fairly short time, we each had a bowl of soup, a hunk of bread, and orders to get some rest, because come morning, we would be working hard. Doing what, we had no idea.

After eating, I settled down on some wisps of straw in a corner—no beds here—and was asleep in minutes. In the morning I awoke early, relatively refreshed. Guards passed out hot coffee for our breakfast. Were we going to starve here? It was one more thing to worry about. We had been told that the Germans still needed us, and that the Russians were closing in. If both these things were actually true, we had two reasons not to complain.

Then they took us out for our work assignment: digging anti-tank ditches to thwart the advancing Red Army. I suppose there might have been a way for us to sabotage the work, just as there might have been in the factories. But the end of this nightmare felt too close. Everyone wanted to stay alive just a little bit longer, till Liberation. Should Liberation come, that is.

The work was awful. The ditches had to be dug deep, and the ground was rock-hard. We swung picks and shovels for two or three weeks, all under the supervision of some of the nastiest, crudest, cruelest German officers we had yet come across—and that was saying something. Then, after a long day, it was back to the barn, back to lousy sanitation, but at least back to a small meal. We were thankful for food. After so much lack, it took relatively little to make us feel fortunate.

One day, Gestapo officers came in from nearby Chenstochowa to announce that it was time for us to go to Germany to rebuild the Pionki factory there. We didn't mind moving, although we hated the cattle cars. We had been through so much, however, that once again, as long as we didn't go to Auschwitz, which as always meant almost certain death, we could make the best of it. We just needed to hold on a little longer, till we knew if we had been told the truth.

The cattle cars actually weren't so bad this time. Sounds funny, I know, because they were still cattle cars. But with only seventy-five people per car, they were relatively comfortable, even. We could stretch out, the "bathroom" bucket wasn't as horrible as it had been on previous trips, and, most amazing of all, we could enjoy fresh air through the open doors—which of course were guarded by two armed SS guards.

The train started rolling westward. We were headed, we knew, in the direction of Auschwitz. Those who had been chatting quietly in the car grew silent. But when we passed the dreaded camp, we all let out an audible sign of relief. And at the old Polish-German border, many of us sat up straighter, alert to the possibility of something new. The question was, was it going to be worse in Germany than in Occupied Poland, or would it be better?

After a while, the train turned north. We stopped to get some water and relieve ourselves outside, under the careful eyes of the guards.

The next day, we passed through Berlin, the capital of the Reich. Because the doors to the boxcars were open, some curious onlookers glanced our way, and once in a while we locked eyes with them. What must they have thought of us, filthy, skinny, in our shabby clothing? And how strange it was for us, to see ordinary Germans minding their own business, instead of dreaded German soldiers!

We chugged on for another hour or so, till we came to a station with the big sign Oranienburg-Sachsenhausen. The camp of Sachsenhausen was famous. Built in the late thirties, it was one of the first of the prison camps, and held mainly German political prisoners, as well as Roma (Gypsies), homosexuals, Dutch, Norwegian, Jehovah's Witnesses, and others. It was not only the headquarters for all the Nazi camps, but also the training grounds for all the SS guards. Although primarily a labor rather than a death camp, Sachsenhausen was still the site of many executions, however.

We stood on the cobblestoned platform while the few females among us were separated off to the women's camp of Ravensbruck, just over thirty miles away. Then we men were in for a few hours' wait. It turned out that the camp didn't want "dirty-Polish-Jews-bringing-in-typhus." They had gotten rid of their last remaining Jews in 1942, when they sent them all on to Auschwitz.

But somebody must have contacted a higher official, who knew that we dirty-Polish-Jews-bringing-in-typhus were good workers, and they informed the camp officials that they had no choice but to take us. At last we got the order to march the short distance through the town to the camp. This time, it felt like no one wanted to look at us. When we reached the attractive, two-story, whitewashed building that marked the camp entranceway, we continued through two columns of SS guards wielding bayonets. That was almost funny, actually. It felt as though we had an honor guard.

Then I looked up to see the big block letters above the gates. *Arbeit Macht Frei*. Work Makes You Free. It was the first time I had seen those words. It would have been nice had the Germans really meant them.

The first thing that happened to us in Sachsenhausen was the anti-lice routine, starting with the head-to-toe shave and shower. We were used to this by now. Still we never trusted, even in a labor camp, that we wouldn't be standing naked under a showerhead and be inundated with lethal gas instead of water. But when the moment came, we once again welcomed mayim. Water. Although we didn't sing, it was still a relief that I cannot overstate.

Next came the valuables search in all our body cavities, a much more unpleasant routine, followed by disinfectant spray. After the close shaving job they gave us, the sting of the DDT on our skin was not to be believed. At least the striped paper pajamas we received afterward were not as rough on our sensitive skin as they might have been, small mercy that that was. When we were dressed, we walked barefoot out the door to get registered.

There has been much talk of prisoner tattoos in the camps, but for some reason we didn't get them, although we did get numbers. They started our group with 96300 and went up from there. Then they told us what was to happen next. Even though we were always spoken to in German, even in Poland, where we never had Polish guards, we could understand what was said to us because Yiddish is so similar. The guards informed us that we would be quarantined in Bloc 55 for three weeks, then sent on to a sub-camp, Glowen, where we would be rebuilding the munitions factory from the parts we had brought.

So we marched to the long, low, brown barracks. Along the way we looked at each other and, despite, our situation, very nearly laughed.

"Is that you, Jakubowski?"

"Of course it's me? Who do you think it is? Hitler?"

"Couldn't be Hitler! Not a hair on your head. Or anywhere else, I'll wager."

"And where did you get that terrific suit, Berkowicz? Paris?"

"Have you seen yourself lately? You're wearing the same damned thing."

We were soon met at the barracks by our German bloc commander. By the pink triangular patch on his uniform, we knew that he had been imprisoned because he was a homosexual. That's how we knew everyone's status: the color of the patch. We Jews wore yellow.

This bloc commander demonstrated his personality right away: he was crueler and nastier to us than most of our captors. But his assistant, a Dutch Communist—we knew he was a political prisoner by his red triangle—was even worse. I wondered whether whatever caused him to limp so badly was responsible for his anger. Or maybe he had been a monster in his previous life, as well.

These two lined us up in front of the barracks and told us the usual rules, such as the importance of keeping our three-tiered, shelf-bunks neat, and of getting out on time for morning roll call at the *Appelplatz*. By now I could have recited these familiar regulations in my sleep. We also learned that we wouldn't get much food, or real clothes, or even shoes during the three weeks we were in quarantine, even though it was getting toward fall.

By the time they were finished telling us what to expect, we wondered once again if we'd come here to die.

Chapter 14

What Happened at Glowen?

"Stand up straight! Shut your mouths! What's the matter, you stupid pigs? Didn't those miserable whores you call your mothers teach you how to stand still?"

The icy stone of the roll call area at Sachsenhausen was so cold that my bare feet stung as I stood shivering, waiting once more to be counted. It was all I could do not to lift each toe, one at a time, just to give them a brief chance to warm up a little.

The rest of our bodies didn't fare much better. The thin paper clothing they gave us when we arrived was no match for the brutal winds blowing across western Germany in the early fall. Neither were the meager rations in our bellies.

As I struggled to stand at attention, I looked past the large assembly area to the surrounding rows of barracks, and the barbed wire and guard towers beyond. I saw some Russians with the signs on their uniforms: *Sentenced to death.* Whether the sentence was to be carried out by crematorium, gas, hanging, shooting or some other form of execution, we didn't know. Other Russians, we knew, were being used as test subjects for gas experiments. It should have been a comfort to know that someone had it even worse than us Jews, but somehow it wasn't.

At last the bloc head released us to the barracks. In our hurry to return to the relative warmth, we jostled each other, using elbows, hands and knees to get past. As often was the case, we behaved exactly like the animals we had been reduced to.

Sachsenhausen was so large and crowded, it was like its own city, the kind that draws in people from all over the world and from every imaginable walk of life. Our favorites were the Norwegian political prisoners, who were allowed packages from home and sometimes spared us a few goodies. The French, on the other hand, attempted a revolt, for which they were severely punished. The camp had a special section for dignitaries of all nationalities, including the Austrian chancellor, French ministers and Polish generals, prisoners all. Of course every city has its prostitutes, and supposedly some of the most powerful and wealthiest in camp were allowed to enjoy their talents. And despite the top brass's objection to allowing in Jews, there was even a Jewish quarter: 200 of our people in barrack 18. These were the counterfeiters of documents and British currency, the jewelers, printers, and watchmakers with the skill and dexterity to replicate almost anything.

We did nothing, day after day. And then, at last, just when we thought maybe the Germans had forgotten about us, our three weeks of isolation were over. We were ordered once more to the bathhouse, where we showered and dressed in real clothing, striped shirt and pants, and wooden clogs. Then they marched us back to the station, loaded us onto another cattle car, and we were off again. The ride wasn't so bad, but travel was always a problem for us in those uncertain times, when absolutely anything could happen to us. I guess it's true what they say: the enemy we knew was always better than the one we didn't.

The war was well into its fifth year when we stopped at the sub-camp of Glowen. Glowen was a small camp about seventy miles to the northwest, situated in the middle of a large forest, between the towns of Glowen to the north and Nitzow to the south. We Jewish men, nearly 300 of us, occupied two barracks opposite one another; the third was reserved for toilets and showers. On the other side of the barbed wire fence were several hundred women, Hungarian Jews who had also been sent to the camp as forced labor.

We hurried to our bunks to get some rest before the next day's work began. Although we were expecting some food to fill our empty bellies, all we got was some soup so thin it didn't deserve the name. An oversight, we naively hoped.

The air was cold the next morning, as we made our way, again with nothing but coffee for breakfast, to the huge warehouse outside of camp that housed the materials we had packed onto the trains in Pionki. We trudged through day after day like this as workers for the Dynamit-Actien company (DAG), but we were no ordinary workers. As forced laborers, we were barely fed, and our prison uniforms, although made of cloth instead of paper, were ridiculously flimsy. Somebody finally got the idea of stuffing the empty cement bags into our clothing to guard against the worsening cold.

"What's that you got under your shirt, prisoner?" a guard barked.

"Nothing, sir."

"Pull it up, then." When the guard saw the burlap bag, he ripped it out from under the uniform.

"Don't let me catch you doing that again," he growled.

He didn't catch us, maybe, but we continued to do it. We weren't as afraid of the guards at Glowen. They were Croatian, not as fierce as the Ukrainians had been at other places. And the SS men at the camp were older than we'd seen before. Maybe their hearts just weren't in the torture and humiliation as much as were those of their younger counterparts. Maybe they sensed they too were beaten. Or maybe they were just tired.

We were tired too, and more than that, we were hungry. Thankfully, we were sometimes able to get some food from the company's German employees.

One day, about thirty of us were marching back to camp at the end of a long, cold, hungry workday when we passed a farmer on a small, horse-driven wagon overflowing with beets. We were guarded by three soldiers, but an empty stomach knows no fear. Without planning anything in advance, without even making eye contact with each other, we all jumped on the wagon and grabbed as many of the dirty root vegetables as we could.

Oh, the taste of those beets! Never mind that they were hard as rocks, or intended for animal feed. To us, they were a delectable dish.

No shots were fired; I think the guards were too shocked at our bizarre behavior to think to use their weapons. It took all three of them to drag us from the wagon and force us to return the uneaten produce.

When we returned to the camp, I got fifteen lashes with the whip. It hurt like anything, but I didn't cry out. I just squeezed my eyes shut and thought of those beets. Without a glimmer of regret.

By Christmas 1944, the weather had become unbearable. At the same time, the head SS man in camp stopped by the barracks for a visit, and we even got a little cake. Miracle of miracles, we were also allowed half-hour work breaks at noon, and sometimes one of our young Jewish workers would warble a song to pass the time. As long as he sang the hit song "My Yiddishe Momme," we were permitted to sit and relax a bit. We all grew emotional during these concerts, but no one as much as he.

By the following month, we understood the thawing of the hostility, if not the weather. The Germans were closing up Glowen and sending us back to Sachsenhausen. Many prisoners were sent on to an airplane factory in Rattenah, but the rest of us returned to the main camp with Commander Mendel.

Another move, more uncertainty, and still no word of my family. I climbed into that train wondering for the hundredth time if the Germans were finally going to finish us off once and for all.

I thought about the meaning of that hit song. How the singer had never needed his Jewish mother as much as he did at that moment, how he'd love to embrace her, to hold her once again and repent for anything he had ever done to upset her.

Amen.

Chapter 15

What Led to the Death March?

I could no longer feel my feet, and invisible fingers of hunger were clawing at my insides. For close to two weeks we had been marching, if you could call dragging famished, emaciated bodies marching, and the ditches along the route were strewn with the bodies of the fallen. That first week, anyone who stepped out of line was immediately shot. By the second, however, the guards didn't seem to care as much. That was a good thing, because from time to time some of us would have to stop and peel the bark off the trees or munch on wildflowers or nettles to fill our painful stomachs. Sometimes we were lucky enough to come upon a dead horse and, if we weren't beaten too badly for it, roast its flesh over a hastily built fire.

The air was alive with the roar of artillery, and the roads teemed with refugees and the occasional Swedish Red Cross ambulance—which we weren't sure if we could trust, because the Germans had commandeered them at one point. Approximately 26,000 prisoners left Sachsenhausen for this final death march. On the way, more than 10,000 were shot or simply collapsed and died. In twelve days, our ragged group covered 125 miles. The numbers are awe-inspiring, but the numbers don't begin to describe the misery.

It was January, 1945, and back in the main camp of Sachsenhausen, our stomachs were as raw with hunger as our skin was raw with cold. There were already thousands of prisoners crammed into fifty-odd barracks, many of them Poles and Jews who had taken part in the Warsaw Uprising a few months before. Just when we thought the sanitation and overcrowding couldn't get any worse, they brought in more Jews from other camps. We now slept two to a bunk, and we had even less to eat. The soup was once again little more than faintly colored water, and sometimes there wasn't even enough of that.

Each morning we marched to work somewhere outside the camp, one day repairing the train tracks that the Allies had bombed, the next working for private companies where we made grenades, or airplane parts, or bricks for all the monuments to the so-called Thousand Year Reich—which, we sincerely hoped, would come to an end after only twelve.

By February, the Allies had stepped up their bombing, and our work changed. Now, we were sent ten at a time the twenty-five miles or so to Berlin, to dig up unexploded bombs, a job that no non-forced labor would touch. A trained German fireman actually removed the detonators from the ordnance, but we did the rest.

One day we were digging away when the air raid signal screamed above our heads. Panicked, the guards rushed us to the shelters. As frightening as the bombing was, at the same time we prisoners were thrilled, not only because every hit was a step closer to the end of the war, but because we got a small respite from our harsh labor. We shared the dark, clammy underground caverns with ordinary Germans, businessmen and women in kerchiefs and sensible shoes, their children wide-eyed and trembling. No one spoke to us, and we couldn't blame them, given our dirty faces, our floppy striped pajamas. But a few of them eyed us with interest, as we, surreptitiously, did them.

When the all-clear signal sounded, I saw one harried mother drop a hunk of dry cake she had been feeding her toddler. Quick as I could, I reached down to grab it before somebody stepped on it, or took it for himself. I swallowed that cake so fast that I couldn't say what it tasted like. All I knew was that it was more calories than I'd have the rest of the week. As I passed on to the street, I saw another prisoner palm a cigarette butt he'd found in the shelter. He would undoubtedly trade that back in camp for food. When you're desperate, you do what you have to do.

Another night, the bombs fell so close to camp that the guards in the towers and around the perimeter wouldn't dare cross the wire to get inside.

"You think this means we can do anything we want?" someone asked.

"There's only one thing I want to do," I replied. "Eat."

"Let's do it then!" And with that, we raided the warehouse where the food was kept and had ourselves a feast, with the bombs crashing all around us.

Other air raids did not end so well. One factory took a direct hit from some of the two-pound Allied bombs before the prisoners could be evacuated, and many were blown to pieces. These bombs were set on timers, with staggered explosions. Every time we thought it was safe to go about our business, another one would go off. The best we could say was, at least the British were closing in.

Through it all, the weather just got colder and wetter. Twice a day we stood at attention in the huge Appelplatz waiting for the count. Anyone who annoyed the guards was tortured or hung or sent to the Z barrack—"Z" perhaps for the Zyklon gas they used to execute them. The Jews always got the gas.

And then it was March, and, miraculously, the situation changed with the weather. We heard artillery fire coming from the East, a sure sign that the Red Army was rolling toward Berlin. The British, we knew, were on the move from the West. We also heard rumors that we Jews were going to be separated from the other prisoners. When they counted us, we already stood by nationality, so this was easy to do.

There's an optimist in every group. "Pesach is almost here," this guy said one night. "Like the ancient Israelites from Egypt, we will be redeemed!"

"Either that or the Nazis will finish off us Jews as soon as they can," someone replied. "Maybe drown us all in the Red Sea."

By April, we were no longer allowed to leave the camp, which meant no outside work and plenty of time to worry that we were no longer useful. Every movement of the guards was enough to cause a commotion. The tension was so high that one night, the German bloc elder from our barracks simply up and disappeared, off to join the army.

By this time we had as many as 600 extra Jews in our barracks, most from Hungary, the Lodz ghetto in Poland, or the few survivors of Auschwitz. Those Jews in barrack 18 who had been counterfeiting money were relocated to Austria, along with the tools of their trade. We knew things were getting hot.

Then a close friend of mine from Lodz, David Goldberg, hit on a plan.

"You know these stars we wear?" he whispered to me late one night in the barracks.

"Sure," I said. They were red and yellow Stars of David made from two triangles from different groups. "Nu?"

"Suppose we pulled off the yellow triangle that makes them into stars," he said. "Then we'll just have a red triangle, like the Poles. And we can just—assimilate. At least as Poles we'll have a better chance of coming out of this thing alive."

I'm sure he wasn't the only one who thought of this, but the plan worked brilliantly. The next evening, we heard the announcement over the loudspeakers: Line up six abreast, according to nationality. David and I simply pulled off our yellow triangles and joined the Polish group.

The Polish criminals and political prisoners were smarter than the guards, and they caught on immediately. Needless to say, they didn't like the idea so much.

A harsh voice cried out, "Hey, get out of here!"

Two of them shoved us, hard. "Dirty Jews, go back to your own!"

Just as we started to leave the column, an SS guard approached.

"What's going on here?" he asked, pushing us back in with the others.

Had he waited for an answer, we could have been executed on the spot. Instead, he went on his way, and we were officially Polish prisoners.

It was on a star-strewn night in late April, 1945, that I marched out under the main gate of Sachsenhausen for the final time. Just before we headed north, the guards gave each column of six men a fresh, fragrant, two-pound loaf of bread for what we were told would be a three-day trip.

Never trusting the future, I finished my hunk on the spot.

After twelve days on the march, our small group was sent into a forest to settle in a clearing. Some people drank from a small brook, till the water all but evaporated. Others nibbled at plants. Corpses piled up in every direction.

We knew the end of the war was almost upon us. If only we could make it a few more days! David and I took turns sleeping and keeping watch, so that no one would steal our blankets or shoes. There was so much confusion; I don't know what I would have done without him.

That last night, we didn't dare close our eyes. And so we were awake to witness the strangest thing happen. We saw the guards take off down the road, one by one, some of them dressed in the striped uniforms of dead prisoners. And then, at midnight on May 2, the SS men also disappeared.

My friend and I looked at each other blankly, and then we hugged. There was only one thing this could mean.

We were free.

Chapter 16

What Were the First Few Days of Liberation Like?

The same sun that had dawned on nearly six years of the Nazi occupation of Poland rose over Germany that morning in early May, 1945. Our throats tight with anticipation and fear, David and I crept out of the forest. Most of the others had fled at midnight, but we figured we had waited for freedom so long already, we might as well stay put till we could see where we were going.

When we reached the main road, we spotted German trucks racing out of the area, their tires squealing. We had no idea where we were or what to do. Without any goal other than freedom and food, we simply started walking, and before too long, we came to a simple farmhouse.

We looked at each other. There was no need to speak. We had two immediate needs: sustenance and revenge. I honestly couldn't tell you which urge was stronger in my heart. We banged on the wooden door and opened it without waiting for a reply. Standing in the middle of the floor was a young woman trembling in fear, her arms around her small, round-eyed child.

"What do you want!" she growled, her voice quavering. "They've already been here. There's nothing left." Her voice and words may have been hard, but her moist eyes betrayed her terror.

"Who's been here?"

"Prisoners. Like you. I'm—sorry. I would like to help you, but they took everything. See for yourself."

We were in no mood to do a thorough search. We also found to our surprise that we were also in no mood to torment or kill poor German peasants. Shaking our heads, we left them in peace.

As we returned to the main road, David pointed ahead.

"Hey, look at that!" We had come upon an abandoned German tank.

"Do you think they would have left anything behind?"

"I'd say it's worth a peek inside. After all, they're not as hungry as we are."

Climbing aboard, we located some sugar and cognac. So it was that our first taste of freedom was infinitely sweet. It was too sweet, actually, and too much to handle on our weak stomachs. We only finished a little, and saved the rest for later.

The more we walked, the more German soldiers we saw, racing to the West ahead of the Red Army. Now, it was we who were in control, while they were running for their lives. We grabbed what we could from them as we passed, discarding onto the road anything we couldn't eat or carry.

At last we approached the outskirts of the town of Schwerin, where the Americans were holding German soldiers. Americans! They were taller than we had imagined, and they appeared so strong and healthy in their crisp green uniforms. As they strode around the area, they looked every bit the conquering heroes.

Despite the Americans' best efforts, however, the atmosphere was more like a flea market than a detention center. All around us former prisoners, most of them still in their stripes, were plucking at the German soldiers' belongings: rucksacks, clothes, shoes, anything they could grab, it seemed, whether they really wanted it or not.

The American soldiers tried to stop us, but what were they going to do? Shoot? For us, it wasn't just the items; it was the principle of the thing. We were like children released from a thousand long days of school. I relieved one officer of his leather coat, his watch, and his fancy Pelikan fountain pen. He didn't seem surprised, or even particularly sorry. Maybe he was actually relieved that that was all I did to him.

The Americans were using an old military camp to house former prisoners, turning it into a so-called displaced persons camp. But the sight of guards, even American guards, sent icicles of fear down my spine.

"No more camps," I said to David. "Never."

He nodded. "No more guards. I'm sure we'll find something else. Something better."

And we soon did, a bombed-out house with a missing stairwell to the second floor. By now totally exhausted, we located a primitive ladder to climb up and did the best we could to make ourselves comfortable. Snuggling under my new leather coat, I rubbed the new watch on my wrist, as if summoning a genie from a bottle. But most of my dearest wishes had already been granted. I was sleeping in freedom, my stomach had something in it, and I was one step closer to home.

In the morning, we ventured into town. Schwerin is known for his fairy-tale castle and its network of lakes, and the war didn't seem to have done much damage. We registered at a Red Cross office and took full advantage of the food and care packages they offered.

"Do you have any next of kin who could help you?" asked the nice American Red Cross worker helping me with my paperwork.

I didn't exactly know the term, but I figured it out by the context and told her about my father's brother Ben Rakowski.

She smiled encouraging. "And where does he live? In the States?"

This I could answer without hesitation, from his letters to my grandmother over the years. "Lima."

She frowned. "You mean in Peru?"

I shook my head. How to figure out just where Lima was? With all my might I tried to conjure up his return address, to give her a clue. Then, as if it were a beacon of light in the distance, I saw it: a logo on the envelope.

"Buckeye Reliance?"

Her eyes gleamed. "Buckeye! Ohio! Lima is in Ohio! We can contact him!"

The workers were kind, but try as they might, they couldn't get us to stay in their camps. You would think these good-hearted people would have understood, but really, how could they, when they hadn't had our experiences with wire and fences?

In our weakened state, all that walking was tiring. We returned to our abandoned house and explored the area a little more. In a nearby courtyard, we came upon another little house, this one with an intact room. We decided to stay there for a while and decide what to do next.

"Hello?" Not long after we arrived, we opened the door to two sickly-looking young women, clearly fellow prisoners. David and I helped them inside and shared what little food we had with them.

When they seemed better able to talk at length, I asked, "Where are you from?"

"It depends what you mean," the smaller, darker one said. "From the city of Lvov, or from the camp of Ravensbruch?"

Briefly we exchanged stories, then a silence filled the room.

"So, where are you going?" the other woman asked. "Do you have a plan?

"We're thinking maybe Lübeck," David said. "Anywhere but another camp."

"Lübeck is occupied by the British, yes?"

David nodded. "And it's not far."

"I don't know if I can make the trip just yet," the shorter one said.

I shrugged. "We're in no hurry."

For several weeks we four stayed in Schwerin, eating, getting shaves and haircuts, even occasionally helping the Americans round up some Nazis. One day we were walking through the streets and came upon a Jewish GI from Brooklyn, New York. He told us that his name was Moishe.

"Look," he said, after chatting a bit in broken, strangely accented Yiddish. "Let's get you fixed up."

We didn't know what he meant, but it was such a treat to be in the company of a real American Jewish GI that we didn't protest.

To our delight, Moishe led us to a large department store.

"Go crazy," he said. "Get what you want. It's my gift to you. There but for the grace of God, and all that."

Again, we didn't exactly know what he meant, but we were thrilled to leave our rags behind and emerge from that store looking like new men and women. If it's true that clothes make the man, we were truly reborn.

This may sound hard to believe, but after a few weeks, we were bored. So we made our quick trip to British-occupied Lübeck, which was better set up for survivors than Schwerin. I was hanging around outside the Red Cross office there when I spotted a familiar face. In another moment, I let out a whoop of joy. It was my cousin Arthur Rozenek, from my town! After the initial embrace, I barraged him with questions.

"Where were you held?" I asked. "How are you? Have you heard anything about anyone else in the family? About my parents or brother?"

To my immense disappointment, he knew nothing about the family. Then I heard the rumor that the Americans were moving on. We were asked if we wanted to help them fight the Japanese in the Pacific. Fat chance, as they would say. I felt as though I'd had enough of war to last several lifetimes. We were going back to Poland.

The Russian liaison to the American forces back in Schwerin was a Jew, and he was friendly to us. When we told him we wanted to return home, he offered to take us as far as Kiel. Apparently they were transporting Russian POWs back East from there, and they could drop us off in Poland. So we went with him to Kiel to join the transport.

What a mistake! As soon as we left the American zone, they stopped the train and unloaded everybody. I couldn't believe it.

"What's going on?" I asked someone.

"They're using the POWs to dismantle any equipment that can be shipped to Russia."

"Why would they treat their own men like that?"

"Because to the Russians, anyone captured by the Germans is a traitor."

I shook my head. "What a world."

Thankfully, we Poles were able to talk our way out of the situation, but it took forever, and we weren't sure till the last minute that we'd be allowed to move on. The others had to walk the rest of the way to Russia. I wonder how many of them actually made it.

Finally, we got back on a train, a regular passenger line this time. When we reached Szechin, on the Polish border, we were again stopped by the authorities. I was twenty years old by then, so I had to register for the draft. They handed us identity papers and 200 zlotys each, our refugee pay. Because I had been captured, I was also granted a fourteen-day pass from the army, after which I would have to report for duty.

We were questioned for hours. I dutifully told my interrogator where I had been and what I had done while in Germany.

"And yet you made it out alive," the fat man muttered. "Tell me, did you collaborate with the Germans?"

I couldn't believe it. Without a thought, I spat on his desk.

"Get the hell out of here!" he barked, rising to his feet, his face red.

On my way out, I crumbled up the fourteen-day pass and tossed it into a bin. There was no way I was going into the army. I was going home.

Chapter 17

What Happened When You Got Back to Poland?

Standing in the crowded offices of the Jewish Committee in Krakow on a bright June morning in 1945, I'm sure I wasn't the only one trembling. After all, we were all refugees from the same hellhole; we were all desperate to discover what had happened to our loved ones. We all wanted to go home and resume our lives. But I wasn't paying attention to anyone else, and the peals of surprised laughter and mournful sobs all around me barely registered. All I could concentrate on was the slip of paper on which I'd scrawled the words Lwowska 2 that was dancing in my hands as if it had a life of its own. That was my mother's current address, which I'd just found in the register of people who had passed through the building on their way back into the city.

Mama was alive.

The address was a window into my past. It was the site of my uncle's little factory before the war, and I had worked for his company in another building nearby. I rushed to the apartment, only to be told by the janitor—whom I'd known when I worked for my uncle—that my mother was at the hospital, caring for Aunt Mina.

Should I go to the hospital? Was there a point? After all I might miss her, and I was in no mood to travel across town on such a comedy of errors. I don't remember how long I sat on the front stoop waiting, probably an hour. My anticipation was at a fever pitch, yet somehow I couldn't bring myself to move from the spot. I had learned over the past few years not to trust information I couldn't verify with my own two eyes, and I was more than eager to do that now. Had a young man ever missed his mother more in all of human history? Even the author of "My Yiddishe Momme"? I sincerely doubted it.

Every woman making her way toward me had something in common with my mother: the tilt of her head, the angle of her nose, the rhythm of her footsteps. But none of them was mine. My eyes were playing tricks on me, I knew, and so at one point I shut them as tightly as I could. When I opened them again, there she was, standing in front of me. She was much thinner and paler and more careworn and ragged than I remembered her, but after two years of not knowing if she was among the living, she was as beautiful to me as the film star Marlene Dietrich.

As for her, it took her a second, a fraction of a second maybe, for the war-ravaged guy in the doorway to register as her son. Did my mother cry when she saw me? I have no idea. My eyes were too full of tears to see.

The country was in chaos. There is no other word for it. The Germans had expelled the Poles from land in the East that had been theirs for a century, so the Poles threw out the Germans from their land in the West. At the same time, there were Jews from the Soviet Union pouring in. Everywhere we looked, the trains and trams and streets were overflowing with people, most of them with hangdog expressions and haunted eyes—and nowhere on Earth to go.

My friend David and I had been headed for Warsaw by train, but we were told that since the capital was destroyed, the Jews were being sent to the city of Lodz. No problem, as long as we could make it home eventually. At the station, we learned that we would get everything we needed in the offices of the Jewish Committee, so we took off for there, not knowing where else to go.

Funny thing. One minute David and I were standing next to each other taking turns writing down our names, and the next time I scanned the crowd for him, he was nowhere to be seen. All I could think was that he must have spotted someone from his past and forgotten, in that instant, all about his present. I completely understood the feeling, but at the same time, I never saw him again, and given what we'd shared, I was sorry for that. I would have liked at least to have shaken his hand.

I knew the Jewish Committee would take care of me, but I didn't know Lodz as well as I did Krakow, and Krakow was much closer to home. I had a pass for the trains, so it was easy to go from place to place, although less easy to get a seat among the travelling masses. Watching the familiar landscape roll by through the train window, I found myself thinking, the land hasn't changed, only us. We have changed forever.

At the Krakow station, there was a poster advertising the Jewish Committee, with an address. Skawinsky 2. It wasn't far. When I finally got to the front of the long, snaking line, the woman at the desk asked me about my needs for food and shelter. I talked to her a bit, and, as I turned to leave, I saw the register that led me to my mother.

And now, just a little while later, Mama was standing in front of me.

"Oh my darling, my darling Shmuel!" she cried when she recognized me. At that moment I was almost glad I hadn't found her sooner, when I had had less to eat and looked even sicker and skinnier. We held each other, right there on the street for all of Krakow to see, for a long time. We both knew that such reunions were taking place all over Europe, and by now, no one even noticed.

When I let her go I asked, "Mama, do you know, did Papa and Yulik make it?"

Mama climbed the few steps, pulled out her key, and opened the heavy door to the building before she answered.

Shaking her head, she said, "We don't know. We don't yet know anything about them."

I leaned over to hold my mother again. This time, she didn't hug back quite as hard, as though the mere thought of our broken family had taken the air out of her. We went inside to the small apartment she shared with Mina, and she made me some tea. She told me everything she knew about who had come back, who was still missing. My Uncle Isaac Levenstein had survived the war in Krakow, but his wife Sarah had been sent to the Bergen-Belsen camp in Germany and hadn't yet returned. Isaac had gone to look for her. Another relative, Maury Pontierer, had returned. A cousin, Adam Wolski, was a doctor and army officer in the Polish/Russian Army. A real *macher*, apparently. Mama said I should go and see him, to get some help, or a job, or just to make contact.

In a lull in the conversation, I asked her what had happened to her those last two years.

"From Plaszow, where we last saw you, Mina and I were sent to a camp called Gross-Rosen, on the border," she said. Mama sighed, and that tiny sound represented more than a year of suffering. "We were freed by the Russians in March. How about you?"

I told her where I'd been, and she shook her head in wonder. Then I asked, "What is Mina in the hospital for?"

There was a long silence. At first I wondered if she had heard me.

"We went back to Kazimierza Wielka," she said slowly, looking down at her hands, which were still red and raw from labor.

I brightened immediately. News from home, at last. "And?"

"We went right to the nobleman. He gave us back our family photographs, but to make a living he had to sell the diamond we left with him."

"The diamond." I shook my head. "Too bad. Still I guess it was to be expected. But what happened to Mina?"

"The Poles don't want us there anymore."

."What do you mean?" After all we had been through these last five years, I don't know why I was surprised. I guess I was just still capable of believing the best of people I'd known all my life.

"You don't understand, Shmuel," Mama said. "They've taken our homes. They like having all that land, the nice furniture. They don't want to give them back."

I nodded. "So what happened?" I knew I had asked three times now. I didn't want to force her, but I had to hear the truth.

"One night, some of the Poles came looking for us. We knew what was coming and ran out the back. When she jumped out the window to escape," she winced at the memory, "she didn't land so well."

The news hit me like the butt of a German rifle. All this time I had been dreaming of home. I'd seen myself walk through the front door, pictured myself back at work in the lumberyard. Now that image was melting before my eyes. The realization that we couldn't just pick up the pieces of our old lives was almost too much to bear. Sipping my tepid tea, I struggled to contain my sorrow. Mama had enough reason to be sad without worrying about me.

I stayed at the apartment in Krakow a few weeks, during which I made it my business to talk to as many refugees and refugee organizations as I could to find news of my father and brother. Just like in the camps, the streets and cafes were ablaze with rumors. This one was here; this one was there. Or was he here? At last, someone mentioned that he had seen my father in a hospital in Austria. If he was still there, he had no idea. But at least it was a start.

How was I going to find the needle of my father in the haystack of war-torn Europe? Maybe Adam Wolski could help. And so I took the two-hour train ride to the city of Katowice, where I stopped to gather more information. What I found there was not my relative, but my destiny.

Pre-war Rakowski family, Kazimierza Wielka, Poland, 1926. Front row (seated): Sam. Second Row: Perel Chilowich Rakowski (grandmother), Moshe David (grandfather). Top row: Frymet (aunt), Rita (cousin), Joseph (father), Joseph Banach (uncle). All but Sam, Moshe and Joseph died in the Holocaust. *Courtesy of Sam Ron.*

Rakowski cousins, Kazimierza Wielka, Poland, 1934. Front row: Masha-Dina Banach (cousin). Second row: Yisrael (brother), Shmuel Banach (cousin). Top, Sam. Masha and Yisrael died in the Holocaust. *Courtesy of Sam Ron.*

Sam, age 14. Kazimierza Wielka, Poland, 1938. *Courtesy of Sam Ron.*

Displaced persons, Linz, Austria, 1945. From left: Minna Banach (aunt), Sophie Rakowski (mother), Isaac Levenstein (uncle), Sam, Sarah Levenstein (aunt), Joseph Rakowski (father). *Courtesy of Sam Ron.*

Breira orphans, Marseille, France, 1946. Sam is in front with his arms around a child. *Courtesy of Sam Ron.*

Ayanot, Israel, 1946. Sam is seated, bottom left. *Courtesy of Sam Ron.*

Hadar, Israel, 1947. Sam and Bilha are standing, top right. *Courtesy of Sam Ron.*

Nevatim, Israel, 1947. Bilha and Sam are standing, fourth and fifth from left. *Courtesy of Sam Ron.*

Tal Shachar, Israel, 1948. Sam and Bilha are standing, top left. *Courtesy of Sam Ron.*

Sam and Bilha Ron, Israel, 1949. *Courtesy of Sam Ron.*

Two families, Yarkona, Israel. Back row: Moshe and Shoshana Zehori (Bilha's brother and sister-in-law), Bilha and Sam. Front row: Chaya Zehori (Bilha's mother), Yisrael (Bilha's brother), Eliezer Zehori (Bilha's father). *Courtesy of Sam Ron.*

Sam in uniform, Eilat, Israel, 1950. *Courtesy of Sam Ron.*

Sam at site of end of Death March, near Schwerin, Germany, 1989. *Courtesy of Sam Ron.*

Fiftieth wedding anniversary, Temple Israel, Canton, Ohio, 1999. *Courtesy of Sam Ron.*

The Ron family, early 2000s. *Courtesy of Sam Ron.*

Sixtieth anniversary of liberation of Sachsenhausen Camp, Germany, 2005. With cousin Rela Feldman. *Courtesy of Sam Ron.*

Boca Raton, Florida, 2018. *Courtesy of Sam Ron.*

Sam meets fellow survivor Jack Waksal after seventy-nine years, Boca Raton, Florida, 2022. *Courtesy of Sam Ron.*

The Rons, Boca Raton, Florida, 2022. *Courtesy of Sam Ron.*

Chapter 18

What Did You Do for Bericha?

All across Eastern Europe, Jewish communities were in tatters. I'm not suggesting that others didn't suffer too, but my aunt's experience in our town was for us the rule rather than the exception: with six million dead and anti-Semitism showing no sign of abating, many of our people had no safe place to go, and no one to return to. Apart from that, the disease, starvation, and general misery that so many of us shared made it hard to hold up our heads, to put one foot in front of the other. To survive, in other words, our survival.

When I reached Katowice, I did what I'd done in Krakow, and what Jews were doing all over the country; I went looking for the offices of the American Jewish Committee office. And on the walk over, I did what everyone else seemed to be doing; I scanned the crowds for familiar faces. My old pal Yoshki Boorstein from Dzialoszyce noticed me first.

"Shmuel!" His voice rang out from across the street. "Hay buddy, how are you? How's your family! I almost didn't recognize you! Where were you these last few years?"

Of course he didn't really expect me to answer all that standing on the street, and besides, I had questions of my own. We spent the rest of the day together, catching up.

"And what are you doing now?" he asked at one point, when we'd exhausted the narratives of trauma from our recent past.

"I'm trying to find out anything I can about my father. If he's in a hospital in Austria, like I've heard, then maybe, as an army officer, Adam Wolski can help me track him down."

He thought for a moment. "I've got a better idea."

"Nu? I'm listening."

"Come join me. I'm involved in a rescue mission from Europe to Eretz Yisrael. It'll give you a chance to travel. I go all over the place."

I wasn't surprised. After all, I'd known Yoshki from my years in our scouting organization, *HaNoar HaTzioni*, the Zionist Youth. He was a doer, and he knew no fear. I had always liked that about him.

I scanned the busy café, leaned back in my seat, and said, "So tell me a little about this mission."

He looked around too and leaned a little closer. "Well, of course it's totally illegal. It's people smuggling. That goes without saying. The British made a deal with the Arabs at the beginning of the war for a strict quota on Jewish resettlement in Eretz Yisrael, and they haven't even honored that. But we doesn't have any choice, do we? The world has already shown us that they wouldn't take in a single Jew more than they absolutely had to." I nodded, and he continued.

"The organization is called *Bericha.*"

"Escape," I murmured.

"Exactly. Pity that we still need it now, after the war is over, but that's the way it goes."

"So you smuggle Jews from Europe to Eretz Yisrael."

"In a nutshell, yes. They're mostly young people, but also some families. As it is, they're stuck in these awful displaced persons camps, which sometimes operate in the old concentration camps. Can you believe it? And in some cases, those who live there are not treated much better than prisoners. It's a horrible situation. Anyway, you would be great at this. I just know it."

"So who runs this Bericha?"

"Now the Haganah does. That's the paramilitary organization in Eretz Yisrael, in case you never heard of it. A guy named Abba Kovner started it last year, in Europe. He got a couple thousand people to Romania, but thanks to the quota, that was as far as they got."

I considered. "And I'd have a chance to get to Austria."

"I don't see why not." He took a breath. "Nu? What do you think?"

It was illegal. I could be thrown into a British jail, never to know what had become of the rest of my family. Did I really want to take that risk, when for nearly six years, I, like the rest of my people in Europe, had been a prisoner of the Germans in one way or another? We had suffered abuse, humiliation, and terrible fear. We had lost our families and friends, as well as, in most cases, our homes and belongings and health. Did I really want to put my newfound freedom at risk?

Then I thought: I have just turned twenty-one years old. This is my chance to be a man, to stand up to evil and not only survive, but this time, actually win. This is my chance to right a few of those wrongs.

I clapped my hands and stood up from the table. "When do we get started?"

Reaching up to shake my hand, Yoshki let out the first laugh I'd heard from him all day.

"I'm thinking maybe we should pay the bill first," he said.

My first mission was to take thirty young people about my age from Katowice to Czechoslovakia. We had told the authorities that they were actually Greek, but there was one slight problem: they didn't speak a word of the language. So some genius come up with the idea of having them speak Aramaic, the language of the Kaddish prayer and the sacred volumes of the Talmud. And it actually worked. To the Russian, British and American soldiers, I guess it sounded close enough.

We made it to Prague. Of course I had never been there before, and I was enchanted. It was truly a beautiful city; the war had barely touched the magnificent old architecture, the castle, the stone arch bridge dating back to the Middle Ages, even the Jewish Quarter. More important, we were on our way to Eretz Yisrael. We were ecstatic.

Then we discovered that the British had closed the border between Czechoslovakia and Austria. They weren't stupid, after all. They discovered that Jews were making their way to Eretz Yisrael by going through Austria to ports in Italy. Now, nearly 3,000 Jews were stuck in Prague indefinitely.

The people I was leading were orphans, and they were understandably distraught at the news. They had lost everything, and they saw Eretz Yisrael as a new beginning, a chance to have a life. The situation had nothing to do with me, but as their leader, I felt responsible. I had to do something.

A directive went out in the organization: They needed volunteers to set up a route to Eretz Yisrael that would go through Germany instead of Austria. The news just about broke my heart, since my goal was to get to Austria. But I knew this was important, so along with three other guys, I offered to help.

The four of us arranged to have Czech identification cards issued for transit by train from Prague to the German border, Carlsbad, the last city in the Russian zone. Then we walked across to Germany. From there, we gave them Deutschmarks for train tickets. Half the group went to Munich, the others to Hof. When they arrived at their destinations, they met up with other members of Bericha. It was like handing over the baton in a relay.

Once we saw how well the plan worked, we went back for another thirty people, and another, and another. I did that for two weeks, until one night, when I heard a gruff voice call out to me to halt. My group and I found ourselves arrested by the Czech police.

"You know you can't smuggle people across our borders," an officer said in broken German.

I had to think fast. I knew the Czechs hated the Poles.

"These are Polish Jews," I said. "If they return to Poland, they will be killed. Their families are already gone."

It wasn't working. I could feel it. I dug down deep to come up with another argument. Then it occurred to me: The Czechs were Communists.

"You know these young people are going to Eretz Yisrael to start a Communist-style commune," I said. I told them that the kids would all be carrying a bottle of cognac for bribes—which they readily understood—and 2,000 Deutschmarks for tickets.

This approach went over better, but they were still suspicious. They decided to test out my story.

At the border, the guards checked out every passenger. During the search, they arrested a number of other smugglers. One girl was even carrying money in a tube of toothpaste. I guess the guards were so pleased with the find that they let us pass.

When they saw our group go through, some of the smugglers yelled out names at us.

"Informers!" they screamed, pointing at our people. We didn't care. We had made it across the border.

One of the officials pulled me aside. My heart pounding with fear, I asked, as politely as I could, what the trouble was.

"We hate the Poles, and we hated this lousy war," he said. "How many of these commune builders do you want to bring in at a time?"

I gulped. Thinking fast, I asked, "Two hundred?"

He nodded. "I think we can arrange that."

In the next few weeks, things grew even easier for us. Word got out that the American troops under General George S. Patton, a noted anti-Semite, were mistreating the Jews in the DP camps. A commission was formed to look into the matter, and among the changes it instituted was the order that the Army was no longer allowed to stop the transit of Jewish refugees.

All this was wonderful news, but I wasn't much closer to finding my father in Austria. Then at last I was given a Bericha mission to Linz, in Austria. Miraculously, my mother had gotten there before me, and she had found my father in a military hospital. She also found much of our family, including Uncle Isaac, who had located my aunt.

Reuniting with my father wasn't quite as dramatic as seeing my mother; still we hugged and shook hands and kept touching each other's faces and arms like we couldn't believe our eyes. He was still weak, but he was recovering.

It was at that first meeting that my father told me what happened to Yulik. He had died in a camp, not long before Liberation. Of course I had feared the worst, and I always thought that if I heard that he was gone, I would never stop screaming. Now that I got the news, though, my first reaction was numbness. My second, not surprisingly, was fury. Why should such a good boy be murdered? What kind of world was it? I knew I had to do something to honor his memory. As long as my parents were together, I thought, it couldn't hurt to keep doing the Bericha work. At least I would be doing some good. And I seemed to be good *at* it, as well.

My next mission was to free from a Polish prison two leaders of the Zionist leftist movement *HaShomer HaTsair*. I wasn't happy to return to the country of my birth, but I did what I was told. Wandering the streets of the Jewish community, I hoped I would come across someone who could help me. I didn't know what else to do. One on busy street I came upon Shmuel Buchman, who had changed his name, he told me, to Validamsky and was working at the time with the Polish Secret Service.

"I even have a cross on my wall," he said, with some amusement.

"Look," I said, "I need a favor. I'm trying to get two Zionist leaders out of prison so they can help Jews get to Eretz Yisrael. Is there anything you can do?"

Shmuel thought a minute. "Sure, why not? After all, I may be a Christian now, but I'm first and foremost a Jew."

As it turned out, one of the men had already been freed. Shmuel helped me free the other one and get him onto a train to Munich.

At the station, we shook hands.

"Listen," he said, "I've been thinking. How about a job with the Polish Secret Police? We could work together, maybe helping Jews from the inside. What do you say?"

"Thanks," I told him, "but I'm happy where I am."

Little did I know that I wouldn't be there for long.

Chapter 19

How Did You Get to the Land of Israel?

The first time I saw someone kiss the ground, I must admit I thought she was crazy. She was maybe seventeen, a waif, like so many of the refugees, with stringy blond hair and a coat several size too big that flapped around her like the wings of a giant swallow. But as we disembarked from the Champollion in Haifa, more and more of the young people bent down to do what she had done. I couldn't believe how glad these kids were to be in Eretz Yisrael. On second thought, of course I could.

I had certainly known Zionists while growing up in Kazimierza Wielka, and I met even more going to school in Krakow. And sure, I had been in a Zionist youth group myself, although I must confess, half the reason for that was probably to meet girls. But my family was so rooted in our little town, had so many ties over so many generations, that the thought of moving to the Middle East had not seriously occurred either to my parents or to me. We wished the Jews in Eretz Yisrael well. We had nothing against seeing Eretz Yisrael someday, although, not being religious, we didn't feel the same need to make a pilgrimage there that some others did.

But as I've already said, I had changed, and my feelings about being a Jew seem to have changed, as well. If nothing else, the Germans had taught me that I was a Jew to my bones, to my connective tissue, to my very being. And this was the ancestral home of my people.

I'm not going to say I kissed the ground, but after a while, it didn't seem quite so crazy.

It was March, 1946, when I got word that my next mission for Bericha was to accompany a group of teens to Eretz Yisrael. I wasn't thrilled at first. I was anxious to see my father, who, according to Mama was getting stronger every day in the hospital in Linz. But Austria was stable now, and I knew my parents would be safe until I got back. Meanwhile, Eretz Yisrael had become a powder keg, with refugees begging to enter and both the British and the Arabs still doing whatever it took to keep them out. Eretz Yisrael, in short, was where the action was. I had never thought of myself as someone who looked for ways to help others. I hadn't thought of myself much at all, frankly, other than simply my need to survive. Now, I liked the challenge of my work. More that that, I felt that with every refugee I helped, I was making the Nazis' dream of annihilating us that much more of a mirage. I won't deny that it was also exciting, the thought of going to another continent, and to Eretz Yisrael, at that. Let's see what all the fuss is about, I thought.

I also knew some of the orphans I was going to be responsible for. They had made their way across Europe in stages, and by then I had played a part in many smuggling operations. I liked the idea of helping them complete their journey.

We took a special train to Marseille, in France. There were over a hundred teenagers in my group. At the port, we boarded the Champollion, a French ship built in the 1920s as an ocean liner for the route from Marseille to Alexandria, Egypt. During the war, it had been used as a troop ship, and now many hundreds of French soldiers were onboard, bound for Tripoli, our first stop.

"Where do we go after Tripoli?" one of the kids asked me, as we sat among the baggage for the voyage. That's where the hundreds of refugees had to stay throughout the trip. It wasn't comfortable or well ventilated, but we were beggars, not choosers. The ship was only designed to fit about 950 passengers.

"From there we go to Alexandria," I told him. "Then on to Haifa. Don't worry; we won't stay long in the ports. We'll be in Eretz Yisrael before the end of April."

The boy closed his eyes. "So what's Haifa like?"

"I've heard there are a lot of Arabs there. And it's old. That's all I know."

We let the conversation falter, each wrapped in his own thoughts. Mine were half about the mission, and half about getting back to Europe and my family as soon as possible. And always, always, there was an undercurrent of sorrow about Yulik.

After reaching Haifa on April 24, we got those kids out of the baggage hold under cover of darkness. When dawn sprayed the sky with gold and they saw Mount Carmel for the first time, everyone on deck sang Hatikvah, what was to become the Israeli national anthem, as if it had been pre-arranged. Maybe it had. Maybe it had been in everyone's mind for years.

> Our hope is not yet lost
> The hope that is two thousand years old.
> To be a free nation in our land. . . .

The younger ones went right to a boarding school in Magdiel, an agricultural village founded by Jews from Europe, located about an hour southeast of Haifa. The oldest kids went to Kfar Usha, a kibbutz north of Haifa in the Western Galilee that had been established by my old HaNoar HaTzioni youth group. The girls aged fourteen to sixteen went south to an agricultural school and community called Ayanot.

I had planned to go directly to Kibbutz Tel Yitzhak, because I knew some survivors from Krakow who had settled there. Before I could arrange the trip, however, the principal of the Ayanot school, Mrs. Rudelson, took me aside.

"Young man," she said with a sweet smile, "I wonder if you'd do us females a big favor."

"If I can, sure."

"I hate to bother you, but I've been watching you, and you are obviously very capable. Also I notice that your Hebrew is really good. I wonder if you wouldn't mind going to Ayanot with us for the weekend? Just to work with the other young men to help the new girls get set up?"

I swallowed, hard. I was learning that I wasn't so good at saying no when someone needed my help. Nor did I necessarily want to. But still.

"Well, I'm sort of on my way to Tel Yizhak," I said. "I've got old friends there."

She brightened. "Perfect! It's just about half an hour from Ayanot. You can get there Monday morning, no problem."

And so I accompanied the group to Ayanot. It's not like they were going to worry about me in Tel Yitzhak if I didn't turn up for a few more days.

There were 200 girls at the school, and just five males to help out with the heavy lifting. I settled in for a weekend of volunteer work. Unloading luggage, building furniture, whatever they needed. And then a funny thing happened. Walking around the grounds, I found myself starting to get interested in this agricultural work of theirs. I knew that plenty of Jews were training in agricultural schools at the time, either learning how to drain swamps or how to grow things in the desert. Things I didn't know a bit about. But now I saw the plowing, the irrigation, the milking of the cows, even how much security they needed against some of their neighbors. It all looked pretty interesting. So much so, in fact, that when Mrs. Rudelson came up to me at breakfast Monday morning, I was prepared with a reply to what I knew full well she was going to ask.

"Shmuel," she said, sitting across from me at the long dining hall table with her cup of coffee, "would you consider staying with us a while longer? The girls feel safe with you, and you're a fantastic help." She paused. "I will pay you a little too, of course. I'm sure you can use the money. Plus you can work six hours and study whatever you want for another two. And if you need extra pay, you can always work up the road at Beit Ovet. They can always use a hand. What do you say?"

As I say, I was ready. "All I have to my name is a gold watch I 'borrowed' from a German soldier," I told her. "So you're right; I could use the money. But I also like what you do here. Sure, I'll stay on for a while."

"So it's settled then," she said with a satisfied smile. She put out her hand. "Welcome to Ayanot. Stay as long as it suits you. A few weeks. A month or two. Or anything in between."

The place ended up suiting me much longer than either of us suspected.

Chapter 20

How Were You Wounded?

When January, 1947, rolled around, I was still living in Ayanot, with no immediate plans to leave. It felt so good to be part of a thriving community again, and even better to be working on something I believed in and could be proud of. It had been a long time since that was the case. Still, when leaders of the Jewish Agency—the primary organization behind the ingathering of Jews to Eretz Yisrael—announced a meeting at nearby Hadar about a new settlement in the desert, I went along with a few guys from the school to see what was going on.

When Mordechai Vasserstrom, Nachum Zachshevsk—one of the document forgers at Sachsenhausen—Yossi Montok and I arrived at that meeting, we were immediately impressed with the level of commitment and thoroughness of the organizers. We were taken with the idea of helping to build the settlement, called Nevatim. I was also taken with a bright, pretty teenager named Bilha Zehori, born and raised in Moshav Yarkona, an independent agricultural community in the area. I knew from the beginning that we would become fast friends. At sixteen, she was too young to think of in any other way. But she had already had quite an interesting life, having been trained for two years already by the Eretz Yisrael fighting force, the Haganah. She understood us refugees, too. During the war, she had lost all but one member of her family in Russia and Ukraine. And now, she planned to teach all of us Hebrew.

The group decided to meet on a regular basis, and we named our small group "Ofek," meaning horizon. *If you will it,* wrote Theodore Herzl, the founder of modern Zionism, *it is no dream.* We knew that our destiny was right over the horizon, and that it would become a reality thanks to our commitment and hard work.

By June of that year, thirty of us were ready to join the settlement, which had been founded by eleven Hungarian Jews the previous fall, on Yom Kippur. Those initial settlers were going elsewhere, and we were expected to build on what they had started.

"Yom Kippur?" I asked their leader over supper that first night. We had just made the long trek to the Negev desert, a few miles south of the city of Beersheva. "Why Yom Kippur, of all days?"

The guy laughed. "For one thing, we're none of us particularly religious," he said. "You'll find that many of us care a lot more about Man than about God."

"That suits me fine," I said. "That's how I was raised."

"Anyway, the British know all about Yom Kippur. They know it's the holiest day of the Jewish calendar, that our people tend to fast on that day and spend the day *davening* in shul. They would never suspect illegal settlement activity on such a sacred day. So we got away with it. By the time they noticed what we'd built, it was a done deal."

"Clever," I said. "We're going to need brains like that."

"You've got plenty of your own," he said. "I hear you've already been elected *mazkir* in my place."

I groaned, mostly in jest. "The first time I was ever in charge of something, and it's a whole settlement. Now I can't complain about anyone else's mistakes."

"*Mazel tov*," he said, with more than a trace of irony. "Congratulations."

"And all for the same slave pay that the Jewish Agency pays everyone else here."

He patted me on the back. "Don't worry, Shmuel. I can tell already, just by talking to you. You'll do just fine."

I hoped so. I looked around the grounds the next morning, taking in the two-storied concrete block tower and the barbed wire perimeter, reaching as far as the eye could see. I knew what we had to do first. We all did. Drill for water.

With the equipment we brought and more we had on hand, we drilled down more than 150 feet. Unfortunately, we didn't wring much water out of that dry earth. But at least we were able to irrigate some land and, equally important, keep two dairy cows.

We started out full of energy and enthusiasm. To some of us, it was particularly gratifying to have use of ten old Garibaldi rifles and a British Bren light machine gun, in case of trouble. How often in the past few years had guns been pointed at us and at our loved ones! We were allowed to keep the firearms only because someone had convinced the British that we were an auxiliary police station. As in the case of Bericha, you had to be sly in these matters. Luckily, we cared a lot more about these details than the British seemed to.

Little by little, however, the horrendous heat, the lack of creature comforts and the low pay took their toll on some of the former idealists. Nearly half of the group dropped out, off to safer, easier lives. We were disappointed, but we couldn't blame them. On the bright side, the Agency still sent us the same amount of money, so now there was a little more to go around. On the other hand, we didn't have as many laborers, not to mention volunteers for guard duty. Why did we need guards? For a start, out of approximately 5,500 souls in Beersheva at the time, well over 5,000 were Arabs, many of whom hated our guts. And that's just one city.

We didn't realize the full extent of our security problem until the 14th of December of that first year. Every morning, two of us would walk less than half a mile outside the perimeter fence to start the water pump. What the guys found when they arrived that day were 400 Arabs from the city of Hebron, about twenty-five miles from Nevatim. Crawling on their bellies to the settlement with their firearms at the ready, the Arabs managed to badly wound one of the pair, Israel Zonareich. His partner, who fortunately was not hit, helped him back toward the fence.

By then the shots had registered with the rest of us. Nearly the entire settlement was quickly engaged in exchanging fire with the attackers, while someone sent an SOS by telegraph to the Palmach—elite Haganah fighters—stationed in nearby Beit Eshel. Knowing the strike force was on its way gave us hope, but not necessarily luck. I got a few good shots in from the parapet of our compound before I felt a searing pain in my shoulder. I had been hit, and bad. I had never felt anything like it. The problem now was that there were no steps down from the roof. All I could do was hang onto the ladder with my one good arm and make my way down, inch by inch, with the blood dripping down my back and my strength starting to give out. That trip was as scary as anything else I'd done up to then, and that's saying a lot. By the time I got to the bottom I was probably in shock.

To our amazement, the response to our distress call arrived in the form of a Polish-made RWD-13 high-wing monoplane. It was flying the very first combat mission in the history of the Israeli Air Force, which had purchased two of the planes just the month before. At the time, I felt more relief than pride. I guess our luck had changed.

The pilot, Pinhas Ben-Porat, had removed the plane's doors and installed a machine gun, so that he could strafe the Arabs and drop grenades, even seltzer bottles, to create general commotion. The overwhelmed attackers soon fled, and the plane landed at Nevatim to begin to evacuate the two wounded settlers. Israel went first, because although I was bleeding badly, his wound was far more serious.

Meanwhile two British half-tracks—vehicles with two wheels in front and two continuous tracks in back—arrived to police the situation. One of them carried me to Beit Eshel, where I could begin to receive care until the Israeli plane returned to pick me up and take me on to Hadassah Hospital in Tel Aviv.

"How did you come so quickly?" I asked the doctor, summoning all my strength to speak.

"Funny thing," he replied. "Just yesterday they smuggled both planes from Lod Airport to an airstrip in Northern Tel Aviv. I guess they were being attacked too often to feel it was safe to stay at Lod. Anyway, one of them was in the Negev to take me to tend to the wounded after an Arab attack on a convoy. When the pilot learned that the wounded had already been evacuated, he was about to return me to Tel Aviv when he got your distress signal. Amazing timing, huh?"

"Sure is," I murmured.

All in all, it was a great day for the Yishuv, the Jewish community in Eretz Yisrael, but not so much for the Air Force. The British immediately declared that any Jewish planes operating weapons were from then on to be shot down without warning.

As for me, despite being wounded, I didn't make out so badly, all in all. While recovering in Hadassah Hospital I had one steady, adorable visitor: young Bilha Zehori, from Yarkona.

Chapter 21

Could You Talk About Bilha?

Is it too much of a cliché to say that a young woman was a breath of fresh air? Maybe, but it was also the literal truth. When I was with Bilha Zehori, I felt like I could breathe, like she was exhaling out to me the fresh clean air of a healthy new land, allowing me to take it in and make it my own. After the dragging, ragged, sloped-shoulder figures of decimated Jewish Europe, with their malnutrition and their sorrow, seventeen-year-old Bilha represented all that was strong and proud among our people: the *Sabra*. That's the term for people born in the Land of Israel. It's Hebrew for the prickly pear cactus that grows there. Like the fruit, they are tough on the outside, sweet on the inside.

As for me, I had grown tough on the outside over the past eight years. Was there any sweetness left in me after what I'd been through? Did I ever have any at all? I could barely recall that naïve, coddled teen who had been so proud of his high school uniform. Who hid in a neighbor's house when the Germans marched into our town. Now, at twenty-three, I was a man.

I may have been a man, but I was also someone's son. One day, a man from the Jewish Agency came to visit me in the hospital. I'm not going to say he was angry, but he was certainly put out.

"Jerk!" he said after a very few pleasantries. "Why didn't you write to your parents to say you were okay?"

I looked at him in confusion. My parents? What did they have to do with it? I had been away from my parents for years, and besides, I would only worry them if I told them I was wounded.

I started to say something along these lines, but the man abruptly put out his hand.

"The European papers reported that you died."

In my weakened condition, the sudden rush of blood to my face made me dizzy. "What?"

"Your name was in the papers, and your parents heard about it and were frantic. It seems that your father spent an hour with Rabbi Silver in

Cleveland—that's the head of the Jewish Agency in America, no less—and he got word to me, and here I am."

"Wow." A rush of emotions overtook me: embarrassment, sadness, worry. "Please let them know I'm okay, and I'll write them today."

In response to my letter of apology, my father wrote back that I should come join them in the States. I explained that with people dying to defend this country, it was impossible for me to leave.

After a few weeks I was released from the hospital, but I wasn't feeling a hundred percent. So I went back to Hadar, where I knew people, and I knew I would be well cared for. I also knew it was close to Yarkona, so Bilha and I could continue to get together on a regular basis. In the meantime, I worked for the Haganah, which put me in charge of their growing armory. I was responsible for the grenades, TNT and other weapons used to fight the British Mandate.

I soon learned that settlements like Nevatim were running out of supplies, so the Jewish Agency was on the lookout for drivers to take the trucks filled with food and other basic necessities. I was happy to get out of the warehouse and help, but I had never driven a truck—not to mention that I had no license. No problem. They gave me a huge, old, heavily armored Chevy with an overhauled motor. Not the easiest thing to learn on, but a young mechanic helped me, and before too long, I was ready for my road test. When the Jewish policeman showed up with his clipboard, however, I couldn't go through with it. Was it that I no longer trusted authority figures? Maybe. Or maybe it was just that a road test seemed like a ridiculous formality for a guy driving a truck in the desert to starving people during a war.

"Don't bother me," I told him. "I have no time for this." When I slipped him a little cash, he seemed perfectly satisfied. I had my license. Now, I was in business.

I invited Bilha to join me on my first haul from Tel Aviv to Pardes Hanna, a trip of about an hour. On the way, we stopped to eat at a dairy restaurant in Netanya, a beautiful old beachside town.

"What can I get you?" the waiter asked after bringing our drinks.

I looked at Bilha, and it suddenly occurred to me: *This is our first date. We are going out to eat, a man and a woman.* It was simply that I thought of it, not that it was exceptionally good or bad. It just sort of took me by surprise.

"I'll have the *leben*," she said.

The waiter knew that most people, even young girls, don't normally eat only yogurt for supper.

"And then?" he asked.

"That's it." She folded the menu and placed it on the table. "That's all I want."

I didn't say a word. Maybe she wasn't hungry. Maybe she never ate much that late in the day. Or, more likely, she knew full well that I was hustling, that for me, at least, money didn't grow on olive trees. Whatever the reason, I wasn't going to make a big deal out of it. I just appreciated that she didn't order three entrees.

"You know since I was a little girl, I wanted to be a teacher," she said, after the waiter set down our food on the table. I was glad she was talking. I myself didn't know what to say.

"My teacher for most of school was a wonderful man named Moshe Shlanger." Her cheeks pinkened. "You know, I think I was a little in love with him." I looked up from my plate. "No, no, don't get the wrong idea. He was big and much older and not very attractive. It was just what he taught. From Josephus Flavius to the ghettoes of Europe. He taught us all of it."

I was so taken with her, I didn't know what to say. "Nu? Tell me more."

"I don't think I've told you that we had an assignment in school, to choose an imaginary person in Europe to write to, and we would write letters back from that imaginary person, too. It was how we made a personal connection to the news. We used the war news to give us the questions and answers. Isn't that a great assignment? We learned so much about what was going on that way." She paused, took a spoonful of yogurt and let it melt on her tongue. "I want to be that kind of teacher."

"I'm sure you will, too."

After we ate, we walked out to the truck. I had intended to go right home, but it was a clear night, and the sky was so full of stars, I couldn't take my eyes off of them, except of course to look at her.

She came up alongside me, and I turned to her. Maybe it was just starlight, but at that moment her face looked illuminated from within. Overwhelmed with emotion, I leaned in to give her a kiss. To my delight, she was happy to kiss me back. In those days, a kiss meant a lot more than it means today. For people like us, it meant we were practically engaged.

"You remember the first time we saw each other?" she whispered.

"Of course. I was on guard duty."

She grinned. "You came riding up on a big white horse. I will never forget how you looked up there. So handsome. So strong. So free."

I held her more tightly. This, then, was normal life. I remembered normal life. Normal life meant love and affection and feeling good, at least some of the time. I nearly cried at the thought of how much had been denied to my loved ones and me all these years. I nearly cried at the thought that happiness was here, in my arms.

I was always looking for work, so I also started to do some things for Bilha's father in the orange groves of their community. One evening after supper at their home, Bilha, her parents and I sat around the table drinking coffee. I was remarking how well the fruit was coming along, and how much I liked the area.

"Do you know anyone around here, Shmulik?" Chaya Zehori asked.

"As a matter of fact, the first group of young people I brought from the Champallion went to Magdiel."

"Just a few minutes away," noted Chaya's husband Eliezer.

Bilha gave me a proud smile. "Shmulik saved a lot of youngsters from Europe. With Bericha."

"I think they know about all that," I said quietly.

"Yes, but just the bare bones, you know." Her brow clouded. "You know I'm already a teacher. I'm interested in the stories. In the details. In knowing what went on, so I can transmit it to the next generation. They need to know. Especially about the heroism."

"Heroism?" I scoffed. "I'm no hero, Bilha. It was exciting. Don't get me wrong; it was dangerous. But anyone in my position would have done the same. Anyone who had gone through that hell and could do something to right the wrongs."

The elder Zehoris exchanged a look, but there was no stopping Bilha.

"But that's the thing! You never talk about it. Bericha yes, the camps no. Nobody talks about it! What happened?"

I looked down at my plate. When Mrs. Zehori spoke, I could have kissed her.

"Let him alone, honey," she said softly. "He'll talk when he's ready. I'm sure he's got a lot to work through first."

Almost giddy with relief, I excused myself from the table.

By early May, 1948, we in the Yishuv, the Jewish community in Eretz Yisrael, were at war with the British for our independence. Another man might have been heartbroken at being in the midst of his second war in three years, but this time I was in an entirely different position: I was fighting for what I had come to see as my country. The fact that I had Bilha at my side—not literally; I was a convoy driver; she was a first-aid nurse—also changed the way I looked at things. Sometimes I almost felt like a character in a novel. Was this my life? I could hardly believe it.

Through it all, our love permeated everything we did; not that we were the first or the last to behave that way. Once night a group of us stayed overnight in Kfar Yonah. We were supposed to split men and women into two rooms, but somehow I managed to take one for the two of us. The top brass were furious, of course, but fortunately they didn't find out until the morning. The night was all ours.

After that, we were separated again, but just for a while. We were apart when, on May 14, 1948, the politicians officially established the State of Israel. Tired as I was, I felt as proud for this new country as though I had given birth to it myself. So much has been written about that day, about the political fallout, the attacks and counterattacks. For me, the most meaningful historical document from that time, however, is a personal one. Bilha wrote me a letter, which I have kept to this day. Here is a small part of it.

> Dearest Shmulik,
>
> I hope that this letter will reach you in good health. The news from the Negev is pretty grim. I hear reports of daily bombardments of Nir-Am and Negba. I can imagine your travels from place to place on these dangerous roads without proper food and rest. I worry about you all the time. . . . Many of the boys my age are falling in different battles. . . . In spite of all the pain and sacrifice, we are the luckiest generation. We are making history every day. For so many generations, the Jews prayed for such a day and we had the privilege to see it happen. . . .
>
> I must finish this letter. I hear the loudspeaker outside. David Ben-Gurion is announcing the establishment of the State of Israel. Shmulik, I started this letter in Eretz Yisrael, the Land of Israel, and I am finishing it in Medinat Yisrael, the State of Israel.
>
> With all my love,
> Bilha

I was driving the convoy most nights during the ensuing fighting. That's when the roads were safest. We were not only concerned with the British war machine, but with the Egyptian Spitfires, as well. But one day in June, I had no choice about when to leave. I had to transport a group of soldiers through the Negev right away, and we couldn't wait until dark.

We were rolling along the desert at a good clip when a Spitfire came out of nowhere and shot out my tires. Some of the guys thought I was going to stop, but I didn't say a word. I just continued driving on the rims till I reached my destination.

Another time I was transporting troops down a different stretch of desert. I knew that the Spitfires could only shoot straight down, so I stopped the truck and told everyone to hop out and run off in all directions, so the machine gun fire couldn't get at them. When the danger had passed, I realized that some of the soldiers had hidden under the truck, despite my instructions. Pulling them out one by one, I berated them—until I came across my closest friend from Pionki, whom I hadn't known was still alive. We greeted each other like brothers.

Another time I was sent to Kibbutz Yad Mordechai, which was under siege. I was supposed to evacuate the women and take them back with me to my community.

As I made my way to the first of the buildings, someone called out, “Hey, you! You’re in the middle of a minefield!”

The women in the truck were instantly screaming, and inside my head, so was I.

“Okay,” I said, calmly as I could. “It’s not a problem. I got in safely; I’ll just go out the same way.” And I had the guy direct me back about a hundred feet, exactly the way I’d come.

With all these adventures, it wasn’t just the trucks that were showing signs of wear. It was also my motivation. These were simply too many close calls for my taste. As I had told Bilha and her family, I was no hero. After six months, I had had enough of convoy driving. I made it through the Nazi occupation; I had no intention of dying in the new State of Israel. Not when I had more to live for than ever before.

Chapter 22

What Did You Do After the Israeli War of Independence?

When the Arabs captured the Negev Desert during the war of Independence, our tiny community of Nevatim had been one of the settlements cut off from the rest of the country. As the war ended, it became increasingly clear to the powers that be that there was no need for the outpost. The Jewish Agency, which was responsible for, among many other things, the development of the country, asked us to relocate to a more strategic site. The idea was to provide a buffer that would keep Jerusalem from ever being cut off from the rest of the country. Bilha temporarily joined our group, which by now consisted of immigrants from not only Poland but also Greece and Turkey: forty young people in all. The plan was to build a *moshav*, a semi-cooperative community, at the foothills of Jerusalem. When we arrived, there was nothing but a couple of buildings that had been erected during the night, for safety. We got right to work digging ditches or cooking or whatever our individual responsibilities were. That was the way we behaved. We did what we were told to do to help the country, and so ourselves, prosper.

One evening, after our meager supper, the head of our little community stood up and cleared his throat.

"I've got some news," he began.

"Can't it wait till our scheduled meeting?" someone said. "I'm beat." There was some general murmured consensus.

"Sorry, but it won't take long." We all laughed at this. Everything took long. The translations alone took time. And everyone knows that forty Jews means forty-one opinions.

"Seriously, *chevrei*. I just got word from the *Sochnut*." (This was the Hebrew nickname for the Jewish Agency.) "For our official opening, we're to expect a visit from some dignitaries, including President Weizmann, along with his wife and Henry Morgenthau, Jr. and his assistant."

Everyone knew the name Weizmann, of course, but there was some more whispering as to the identity of Morgenthau. The American philanthropist and former top politician had played a significant role in assisting Jewish refugees while in office, and had taken a strong interest in supporting Israel—which didn't prepare us for the news we were to receive about our little community.

"Okay, so we'll roll out the red carpet," another joker interjected. "Just don't expect us to wash our hands!" Some of the women who worked in the kitchen quashed that idea as soon as it was uttered.

"Is that all?" I asked, with an exaggerated yawn.

"One—more—thing," he said. We all looked up at his strange phrasing. "They are naming the moshav themselves."

Silence.

"But we already agreed!" one of the kitchen workers piped up. "We're naming it after those poor boys who were killed at Nevatim!"

Our leader shook his head, once. "Not anymore."

"So what's it supposed to be now?"

He hesitated a beat. "Tal Shachar."

It took some of us a little longer to do the translation than others. Eventually we all figured out that "*tal shachar*" was Hebrew for "morning dew," which translated in German to—you guessed it—Morgenthau.

Pandemonium reigned.

Life in Tal Shachar was every bit the struggle it had been in Nevatim, and then some. At least in Nevatim there was a community before I arrived, even if nearly everyone had left. Not to mention the fact that although Bilha came to visit as much as she could, I missed her terribly when she was back in Yarkona. By that time we knew we planned to marry, and she had already made it clear that she had no intention of living in an agricultural community such as the one where she'd grown up. Her mother had warned her when she was small that such a life was too hard and unrewarding for such a smart girl, that she should get a job, maybe teach. And the older she got, the more Bilha knew she was a born teacher.

By the spring of 1949, it was all just too much. Many of the Poles, especially, started questioning our future. I was the last to leave. Finally I schlepped through the mud five long miles till I reached the established kibbutz of Hulda, where I hitched a ride with a truck driver. My destination: Yarkona and marriage.

Our wedding, on October 5, 1949, was a simple affair, although I must have shaken hands with about 500 people. I was sad that my parents couldn't be there with us, but they did manage to call long distance and give us their blessing. Their absence was the only blot on the happiest day of my life up to that point. To my astonishment, this was even better than Liberation. This was belonging, to a country, a family, and, most importantly, a woman.

In honor of the momentous occasion, I decided to legally change my Polish surname of Rakowski to the new Israeli name of Ron. All the immigrants I knew and plenty of those I had never met were doing the same.

It was only fitting. After all, I was a new man. And it was my way of saying I was proud to join the Zehoris by giving their beloved Bilha a new Hebrew name.

I was thrilled to join Chaya and Eliezer's pioneer families, although I will admit it took some adjustments on my part. Although no one gave me a hard time, these Israelis were a totally different breed from the Jews I grew up with: tougher, more sure of themselves, quicker to take action. But I coped. A short time after our marriage, I joined the Yachin orange import and export business, and soon became manager of the packing house, then the main office manager, and the manager of the buying department. It helped that I knew a little English. Meanwhile, Bilha was teaching, and we were both politically active in the Mapai party. It was a very happy time.

Then the Army informed me that I didn't have enough months of service under my belt, so I went back in the spring of 1950. It was orange season, so they let me finish my work for Yachin first before going back in. I did well in that company; my parents had trained me to be responsible, both as a worker and as an older brother. If I was no longer able to maintain the latter role, I put myself into the former with full force.

I was stationed for a while at the British camp of Sarafand, where I fulfilled my obligations to the brand-new Israeli Army by driving trucks. As long as I was safe, it was fine with me.

Chapter 23

What Happened to Your Parents Directly After Liberation?

When my parents were liberated, my father, who had barely survived Matthausen, was sent, half-dead and virtually toothless from malnutrition, to a military hospital in Bad Goisern, Austria. He was treated there from April 1945 to June of the next year. My mother had been in the Grosse-Rosen camp, which meant she had fared better. That's because since 1942, the camp's inmates were prized as slave labor to the German industries supporting the war effort, including such well-known names as Krupp, Siemens, IG Farben and Daimler-Benz. So, my mother, four years younger than my father, spent most of the war reasonably healthy, keeping her, unlike so many others, from the so-called invalid transports to the death camp of Dachau.

One day, somebody in the hospital mentioned to my father they had seen me. He told me later that at that very moment he took off all the tubes and began to eat. He didn't want to be on an IV when we were reunited.

When my parents found each other again in Austria, they wrote me a letter. They were ardent Zionists and had written that they longed to join us in the Eretz Yisrael, but weren't sure it was for them. What could I tell them? At first my heart soared. I missed them terribly. Besides, we needed every able body we could get to populate and fight for the land. But they weren't exactly able-bodied pioneer material. I was young. I could live with danger and discomfort. But them? How could I see them put through the least bit of suffering, after what they'd been through in Europe?

I would love you to join us in Israel, I wrote back, *but right now I have no way to support you. You need to go to the U.S. Come to Eretz Yisrael later. It's better for everybody this way.* After all, I figured, why would they want to be anywhere but what was widely considered the wealthiest, freest, and safest place on Earth? America wouldn't take the Jews of Europe when we were in dire need, it's true, but at least they would take us now. They owed us that much.

After Papa was released from the hospital in 1946, they remained in Austria, living for a time with other camp survivors in a displaced persons camp in the Linz area. The accommodations were grim, however, and the refugees rebelled against being placed in former concentration camps or in temporary barracks. Then, with the creation of the Bindermichl camp, they were relocated to requisitioned housing with 2,500 others, including several of our relatives, such as Aunt Mina, Uncle Isaac Leventsein, Sally, my father's sister Aunt Linny, and many friends. Camp 64, as it was called, had been a beautiful Nazi neighborhood until the U.S. Army kicked them out. Now, it was a hotbed of Zionist activities and political protests against the British policy on new Jewish settlement in Eretz Yisrael. In fact, many of the new camp's activities were geared toward preparing people to live there.

But my parents had other plans. They took my letter to heart. As much as they supported Zionist causes, they were worn out. All my father, especially, could see for himself after the terrible war years was a middle age that wasn't quite as harsh as building a new country out of swamp and desert. Because of my mother and aunt's horrifying experience back in Poland, they knew there was no going back to their old life. So they didn't have a lot of choice. They needed family. They needed safety and stability. They decided to join Papa's older brother Ben in the United States. They arrived in Lima, Ohio, in January, 1947.

So it was that when my father recovered, my parents moved to the United States. They were lucky to have a sponsor. My uncle Benjamin Rakowski had gone to America in 1908, and because of that decision, not only had he completely missed the terror and torment that we had lived through, but his family was also healthy and whole. Ben had emigrated after being involved in a failed attempt—during the time that Poland was occupied by Russia—to assassinate the Russian tsar's four-year-old son and heir. He eventually built up a profitable rubber factory in Lima, and by the time my parents landed, Ben and Jenie and their daughter Helen were more than comfortable, and happy to take them in.

The Rakowskis treated my parents well, and they were grateful. But after a while, Papa knew it was time to move on, to strike out on their own.

One night, my father and uncle were up late chatting and drinking at the kitchen table. My parents had just returned from a short visit to Canton, to visit my mother's sister and her husband, the Trigers.

"So what's doing with your brother-in-law Philip?" my uncle asked in English, pouring a little more Scotch in his glass.

"Good." He continued in Yiddish, "He says he can get me a job in a barrel factory for a while, just for a start."

My uncle looked up from his drink. "Try to speak English, will you? At this rate, you'll never learn. Anyway, a job? Why in the world do you want to work in Canton? That's a couple hundred miles away! There are plenty of jobs here."

"We were thinking we'd move there," my father said with a shrug.

The brothers hadn't seen each other in nearly forty years, but Ben knew a determined man when he saw one.

"You know you're always welcome to stay." He sighed. "Plenty of work for you in my shop. Plenty of room for you here in the house."

Papa nodded. "I know. Thank you. But we've got to make our own way. We don't want to overstay our welcome. How long can I borrow your clothes, sleep in your bed?"

"Family is family."

Papa put out his hand. "And we are grateful to you. We'll always be family."

Our cousin Sam Banach had traveled with my parents to Ohio, staying with Jenie's sister Helen. Sam was nothing like the Old World refugees of my parents' generation. At age twenty, he hit Lima like a spitfire, handsome and dangerous. He learned English overnight, it seemed, and soon adjusted to American culture as though he'd been born into it. It wasn't long before he was driving a Buick convertible around town with a different woman beside him every night. My parents had no worries about Sam; that was for sure.

Meanwhile, they were adjusting to life in the States, albeit a little less quickly than Sam. Thanks as always to family, they found their way. They rented a small apartment in Canton, and my mother, who hadn't worked in Lima, soon got a job sewing buttons for the Burlington Company. In fact, I took Bilha on our leben date with the first ten dollars Mama made, which she immediately sent to me. My father had started out working in America as a laborer. But soon, despite not having mastered English and carrying his dentures for safekeeping in my mother's handbag, he got a decent job with the Timken Company, a major manufacturer that had moved to Canton half a century before. Then, little by little, he got started in what was his real vocation, developing property and building houses.

We learned all this from letters. Once we visited in 1951, however, it was hard to leave. For one thing, the trip was long and expensive. For another, America fascinated me. What's more, it was clear that my parents wanted us close, and, although I was by then a husband and father, I found it impossible to refuse their request. During our 14-month visit, I began to work with my father in his fledgling home development business. He had always had a knack for business, and he certainly understood about building houses.

It was strange to be in this shiny new land, with people who had little-to-no idea of what we had been through. Wartime Europe was like another planet from this land, even, it seemed, for many of the American veterans. Not that my English was good enough to talk to them at the time, but I could sense it. We were as full of hope as these Americans were, but our hope was tinged with sorrow, with loss, while theirs, it seemed to me, was whole and pure.

Still, hope was hope. And while especially Bilha had no intention of staying away from Israel for too long, we appreciated the good life we found in Ohio. And I was overjoyed to be working with my father again. I won't say it was like the old days back in Kazimierz Wielka, though. It was better. It was a gift I never thought I'd have again, something I never for a minute took for granted.

Chapter 24

Could You Talk About Coming to America?

For the first time in many years, I was completely happy. In September, 1950, I was a twenty-six-year-old soldier in the Israeli Army when our beautiful Tamar was born. The only blot on the landscape of my bliss was the fact that I was so irritated that they wouldn't let me in the hospital room with Bilha during the birth. It's a miracle for any loving couple to bring life into the world, but for us, it was doubly poignant. Had we been in Kazimierza Wielka at the time, I thought, this all would have happened at home. But of course I would have been married to a different woman and had a different daughter, and that was simply unthinkable.

So was the war, in those heady days. Mostly, by unspoken agreement among non-survivors and survivors, the darkness of those years receded further with every day of shimming sunshine in the State of Israel. No one wanted to hear about it, which was usually okay, because no one really wanted to talk about it, either. Those who did were generally treated with disrespect, and were sometimes called *sabon*, or soap, a reference to the use to which the Germans were said to have put Jewish bodies. The idea was that Jews in Europe somehow let down the team by not resisting enough, not being as strong as these hearty, Yishuv-born Jews were. When I heard such sentiments, part of me thought, I'd like to see *you* confront a guard with a rifle when you were sick and starving to death. But mostly, I just let it go.

My parents were always asking to see the baby. Back then, a trip to the U.S. from Israel was a major undertaking, and we weren't about to go for just one or two weeks. But finally, in May of 1951, we took a ship to America, and we spent over a year with my parents in Canton. Of course I had been in Krakow, which was a much bigger city than my hometown, but I wasn't quite prepared for the newness and freshness and sheer size of everything. And Americans? I have a feeling that even if I had known more of the language when I arrived, they still would have seemed like extraterrestrials. So open and free! To my eyes, even the oldest among them seemed younger than the youngest survivor.

Bilha and my mother cared for Tamar while I helped my father in the business. Life was good. We were once again surrounded by family, although not as many as we'd had back home. Little by little, the private jokes, the family stories, they all came back to us as though from another lifetime.

One night, the family was sitting around after supper, and someone said something about my Uncle Isaac Levenstein.

"That one!" a cousin scoffed. "He spent the war with Schindler in paradise!"

So the war came up from time to time among us, but not a lot. Even back in Israel we had known people who were participating in what came to be known as "Shoah Business"—the intense involvement in all things related to what they started to call the Holocaust—first and foremost, discussing it. It wasn't that we had anything to hide, either from each other or from the outside world. It was just that in our family, we all knew, either intimately or in a general sense, what we had withstood. America symbolized health and hope and above all freedom. Why go back to those terrible times, even in our heads? Why bring them back to life, either for ourselves or for anyone else? The past was best forgotten and gotten over, like a terrible cold. That was more or less the way we felt back then.

I felt that way about war reparations, too. It took me a long time to sign up for them, partly because I didn't want the German blood money, partly because in America, I didn't need it. Eventually, a lawyer convinced me to apply for a check for about $5,000, or 9,300 Deutschmarks. The fee was determined by how many months I had been deprived of freedom. My parents, because they became seriously ill, were eventually receiving monthly checks that totaled a lot more. My father never fully recovered from starvation and overwork—he was eighty pounds when they picked him off the garbage heap of Mauthausen—while Mama contracted what was later diagnosed as lymphoma from working with toxic chemicals for one of the companies that hired slave labor in the Gross-Rosen camp. They were also able to get $3,500 for their confiscated home. My father was nothing if not a fighter. He was once again very active in his Zionist organization. And one of his major priorities was to get a judgment against a man named Frankovich, who had murdered my Aunt Frymet back in Poland. At that he was also successful.

How were my parents able to get what they needed? Mostly because in 1961, the world was ready, or was forced, to react as one to the enormity of our experience. Adolf Eichmann, one of the prime architects of the Final Solution, the systematic decimation of our people, was captured in Argentina in the spring of 1960, and his widely televised trial began a year later. By the time he was hung in Israel in the spring of 1962, the doors to our secret memories were springing open. People suddenly wanted to hear our stories, and slowly, slowly, more of us began to tell them.

It even happened to me. As much as I had been determined to focus on building my family, my business and my new life, as much as I had been determined not to look back, when someone asked, it was like a fire hose inside me had been turned on. I began to speak at schools, synagogues and community meetings. I spoke to strangers, friends and relatives. Once the hose turned on, it took strength to turn it off again. The world had to know.

But I'm getting ahead of myself. Visiting my parents in the early 1950s was wonderful, but Bilha missed her own family, not to mention Israel itself. We returned and settled in Kfar Saba, where our son David was born in October, 1954. We thought we would stay there a while, but if I had learned anything in my life, it is that God, or whoever it is, laughs when men make plans.

One day my father called, which was rare; we usually wrote aerograms.

"Wow, what a treat! How are you doing, Papa? Is everything okay?" It was my standard telephone greeting, and I expected the standard reply: *Everything's fine by us; we just wanted to hear your voices.* But his response took me by surprise.

"Not so good, Shmulik. To tell you the truth, I am not doing so good."

"Do you—are you saying you need us to come?" Across the telephone wires, I could imagine my father's pinched, unhappy face, unwilling but forced to speak the inevitable.

"Yes, son. I know you've got your life, your family. But that would be a great help, if you could come work with me."

How could I say no? That is how we found ourselves returning to Canton in 1955. This time, it was not just to visit, but to stay.

Chapter 25

Did You Encounter Anti-Semitism in the U.S. After the War?

"So my best advice to you in terms of getting your green cards is that your wife needs a good, steady job."

The spicy scent of my Cleveland lawyer's expensive cologne wafted toward me from across the heavy desk. I looked around his well-appointed office; the tasteful, comfortable furniture, the subtle lighting. I heard the low buzz of activity in the waiting room. I trusted this guy. He seemed honest, and he had done well for himself, and so far he had done well for me. What's more, I knew that Bilha would be delighted to find a full-time teaching job. She would have preferred teaching in Israel, but my father needed us, and she understood she would have to work in the area, at least for a while. The question was where.

By 1957, we had been in Canton more than a year, living with Tamar and our newest baby David in a cute little apartment owned by my parents. My father's company didn't deal with commercial development, only homes. What with the G.I. Bill that guaranteed many veterans low-cost mortgages, and the post-war baby boom that encouraged families to buy houses, we were doing better than we'd ever imagined possible. I was also taking English classes. I got along fine with the laborers and the customers. And I was glad to be able to help my father.

It wasn't long before Bilha, whose credentials and command of the language were excellent, found a job in Akron, an easy commute of less than twenty-five miles to Canton. The town was growing fast, thanks to its prime industries: rubber and tires. The makeup of the community was diverse at a time when I had read that a lot of the country was not. It seemed like a perfect location for a growing family, with rolling hills and the Ohio and Erie Canals traversing the city.

I knew I would build my own home someday, but our little family needed something right away. We soon found ourselves a house in a decent, middle class neighborhood, surrounded by Irish and Italians. We made no secret of the fact that we were Jewish; both Bilha and I were proud of our roots and instilled that pride in our children. Quite by chance, we had a Jewish next-door neighbor. Or maybe it wasn't by chance. You never know where realtors will steer you. Especially back then, when hotels and clubs were still restricted against Jews and Blacks.

Eventually we moved to Akron, and in November, 1961, Bilha gave birth to our third child and second beautiful little girl, Daphnae. The doctors told us early on that this baby wasn't moving like other children, and she was eventually diagnosed with a mild case of cerebral palsy. We were heartbroken that she would have such challenges in life, but at least we had the comfort that where we were located, she was able to get the best of care.

And so the years rolled by, season upon season, year upon year.

Through all my business and personal dealings, I never hid the fact that I was Jewish. Most of the people I worked with were Italians, Irish or Polish people from the trade unions. I never had a problem with anybody, even when they made little jokes at my expense. Who cared?

One day, I was talking to some of the men on a job site when someone called out, "Hey, Ron, is it true that you people bury bodies standing up?"

I winked. "You have no idea," I said at last. "When I go, I'm going to take a pillow, stuff it with hundred dollar bills, and take it with me." Everybody laughed and went on their way.

I won't say it always worked out so well, though. We Diaspora Jews have our own rituals on Christmas. They've got nothing whatsoever to do with celebrating the holiday, at least not for most of us. These rituals are more about being with family or friends when the vast majority of our acquaintances are enjoying their own. For us, the ritual was to go to our Jewish neighbors' house. When the kids were old enough to know where we were, we started to leave them at home. In those days, nobody thought a thing about it, all the more if the parents were close by, and if at least one of the children was of a responsible age. Or so we thought.

I don't know what time it was that Christmas night, maybe eight o'clock, when we heard a loud banging on the door. Then the doorbell rang, several times.

Our friends stared at one another. The husband sighed, as if maybe he knew what was coming. He set down his drink, rose slowly to his feet, and, despite the ruckus outside, took his time getting to the door. He peeked out the window, then stole a bemused look back at us before opening up.

"What can we do for you, Mrs. M__?" From where I sat, I could see the woman from across the street standing on the top step, her red face twisted into a mixture of contempt bordering on fury.

"Don't your people know you shouldn't leave children alone at night?" she snarled. "I should call the police on the Rons for child neglect!"

I stood up and strode to the door. "Thank you, Mrs. M___, and Merry Christmas to you!" Somehow we managed to close the door in a way that didn't seem like slamming it in the woman's face, but that was what I wanted to do.

We shook our heads and commiserated about the fact that we hadn't left anti-Semitism behind in Europe. I didn't think much of it until a couple of days later, when I returned home from work. I opened the car door, stepped onto the driveway and spotted the same neighbor's teenage son in the street.

Before I could turn my head, I saw him hold his nose. As I looked back at him, he called out, "Stinky Jews!"

I had had enough. It was as if the twenty-five years that had passed since I was back in school in Kazimierza Wielka, with the anti-Semitic kid and the inkwell, had been but the blink of an eye. I'd like to say I thought in that instant that after what my people, my family and I had gone through in Europe in the 1940s, I was consciously drawing a line in the sand. *Never again.*

But it wasn't that way at all. I was just angry. This was my neighborhood, I was an adult, and this was a punk kid who was learning hate at home. I dropped my briefcase, made my way toward him in two long strides and grabbed him by the shirt collar. Or maybe it was the neck. Or both.

"One more time you say this," I snarled, "and I'll kill you. You hear me?"

The kid must've thought I'd go like sheep to the house. His eyes wide, his face bright red, his jaw hanging, he simply nodded and took off like a lightning bolt for home.

I entered the house, briefly mentioned the incident to Bilha and put it out of my mind. We sat down to dinner. Some time later in the evening the doorbell rang, and I rose to answer the door. It was the kid's father, looking exasperated and exhausted, as I was, with neighborhood hijinks after a long day at work.

"What's going on?" He asked. "What happened today with my kid? He's screaming bloody murder!"

I opened the door a little wider. "Come inside," I said. "Let me tell you a story."

It's not that I knew the guy well, but we had been living across the street from each other for a while by then. We had waved when we made eye contact, and we had occasionally passed the time of day. He seemed like a decent enough guy, a hard worker who just wanted to be left alone.

Now I led him into the den and pointed to an easy chair.

"Take a seat. What would you like to drink?"

Over good Scotch, I laid out the Christmas occurrence and the day's events as plainly as I could. I knew enough not to criticize a guest in my house, but I had to be frank.

"I don't know what to tell you," I said at last. "Your wife is an anti-Semite. She's teaching your son to hate."

My neighbor leaned back in his chair and shut his eyes. When he opened them, he leaned forward in his chair and drained his glass.

"How about this," he said. "Give me another drink, and then I'll go home and beat the hell out of her."

I don't have to tell you I didn't like that, either. Maybe it wasn't even true, what he'd said. But I didn't say another word to him on the subject ever again. I didn't have to.

Chapter 26

What Was It Like Being an Immigrant to the U.S. at That Time?

There were days in Ohio in the 1960s and early 1970s when I woke up in the large, sunny four-bedroom house that I'd built on Shannonbrook Street, and I felt waves of joy. If I had believed in God, I would have gotten down on my knees in thanks. Here I was, a successful American businessman. I was president of my Reform temple, and I served on the local Jewish Federation board. Bilha was teaching Hebrew and was very involved in Hadassah. Our social life was active; we had wonderful kids. We had put down good, strong roots here. Even our English was pretty good.

In Israel, I'd picked up modern Hebrew very quickly, because I'd been exposed to the Hebrew of the synagogue all my life. When it came to English, however, the only words I knew were from high school in Krakow, when we learned the lyrics to the British national anthem. Hard to imagine anything more inappropriate in the democratic United States.

> God save our gracious king,
> Long life our noble king,
> God save the king!
> Send him victorious,
> Happy and glorious,
> Long to reign over us!
> God save the king.

That certainly wasn't going to get me anywhere in America. So before we left Israel for the U.S., I took some English lessons, and when we got to Canton, I studied English As a Second Language for a year. By the time I got to Akron, I was ready to enroll in the university. But I had a small problem.

There I was, thirty years old, standing in line among the pig-tailed and bobby-soxed kids at the University of Akron Office of the Registrar. I couldn't help but watch and eavesdrop on them a little, their harmless jokes, their startling innocence. Of course I was much older, with a business, a family, all kinds of worries and obligations. But I thought of myself at age eighteen or twenty, during the war. *It's like we're from different planets*, I mused, not for the first time. *A different species*. These Americans appear so carefree, so full of trust, of hope. I wanted to be like that, too, but if it happened, it was bound to take some time.

At last I reached the front of the line. I held out my registration card to the stern-faced, middle-aged woman behind the counter.

"You are from out of state?" she asked briskly.

"From out of the country. The State of Israel."

She nodded, once. "All right; I need to see your green card." When I didn't immediately answer, she added, "Give me your papers, saying you can stay and take classes here."

"I don't have a green card yet," I replied, trying to look more sorry than I was. After all, we were doing everything we could to get it. That's why we were in Akron. "Isn't there anything I can do until it arrives?"

I held my breath as she considered the problem, all the while tapping her pen against her even white teeth. "Tell you what," she said at last. "Why don't you go see the Dean of the night school. He might be able to help."

The Dean's office was impressive, and so was he. Either he had more important matters to deal with and wanted to get rid of me, or else he really desired to help. I prefer to think the latter.

"I'll sign you up right now," he said, when I'd finished my story. "Then next semester, when you've got your papers, you decide whether or not you want to stay."

I thanked him and hurried out of his office before he could change his mind. Whether in Europe or in Israel, I wasn't used to officials being so eager to help.

The semester began, and I was a good student, taking classes on campus six hours a week and working well into the evenings at home. I studied accounting, economics, geography, and of course English: I was building my vocabulary every day, making enormous progress. It couldn't have hurt that I was already fluent in Yiddish, Polish and Hebrew. Still, English is a tough language. The day of our first test, I sat at my desk in despair.

"Seldom" and "frequent," which was which? "Knight" and "night"—what was the difference? I suddenly understood the English expression "tearing my hair out." I was stumped, and so disappointed in myself.

The next class period, the teacher returned the test papers. I was dismayed to see he had given me a C+. But the teacher had written a note on my paper. I leaned down, eager to decipher the scrawled message.

"Mr. Sam," he had written, "don't get discouraged. If Joseph Conrad was able to write beautifully in English, you can one day, too."

I had to look up the name in the library. Joseph Conrad, one of the most famous Polish authors of his generation, was widely considered one of the greatest prose stylists in English, although he was not fluent in the language at age thirty. He had died just a few weeks before I was born.

In 1963, I went into partnership with a Jew named Ludwig Stern. We worked well together and became friends for life. I also worked closely with a real estate man named Jim Reed. Business was wonderful; we worked around the clock.

I was busy, sure, but I always made time for my parents. They were healthy, considering what they'd been through. But my mother had worked with toxic chemicals during the war, and in 1968 she developed lymphoma. The doctors did all they could, but she died in the fall of 1969.

I threw myself into my work. Over the previous year, I had bought one hundred acres of land next to the fanciest development in the city, where Canton's big shots owned homes. I planned to build a lot of apartments, and somehow these big shots got it in their minds that I was going to rent to the "wrong element," and they sued. On the last day of 1969, the judge called both lawyers into his chambers. He couldn't rule against the big shots, he said; they owned the city. But he didn't want to rule against me, either, an upstanding young man trying to make something out of himself. So he told us to settle.

Through all of this, my father, who had spent a full year in the hospital after the war, had gone in for surgery for gastrointestinal problems and developed an infection. I was visiting him in the hospital in Akron on New Year's Eve while keeping in touch with my partners by phone. At one point they called me and told me we had settled on 270 apartments instead of 429.

If I had ever doubted it, I knew then and there that America was truly a wonderful country, to allow me, a young Jewish refugee new to the city, to prevail over its leaders. The thing was, I no longer cared as much. That night, my father had slipped away.

What do I say about the deaths of both my beloved parents within three months? Does it make any difference that they lived twenty-five years longer than the Nazis wanted them to? After all those years in the States, it was almost as though the long arm of the war found them and swallowed them up. They still died much too soon.

Then, in 1972, both of my partners suffered heart attacks.

I came home after hearing about the second one.

"Bilha," I said, "I know you want to go back to Israel."

She had been marking papers; now she looked up in surprise, her eyes shining.

"You know I do, Sam," she said. "With all my heart. I've wanted to ever since we got here."

I nodded. "Let's do it, then. Life here is good. But I just realized something. I don't want to die here. Let's go back to Israel."

By the time we returned to Israel, it was 1974. Tamar was married and living in Chicago, and David was going to school in Boston. Daphnae was the only child still living at home. I knew moving was a good idea for us, and it wasn't just for Bilha and me. We wanted Daphnae to grow up in Israel. But she needed medical assistance that was only available in the States, so after less than two years, we had no choice but to return to Canton.

Chapter 27

How Was Your First Visit Back to Your Hometown?

Springtime doesn't tend to linger in Canton, Ohio. It always seems as though one day in late March the pale yellow flowers appear on the native buckeyes, embedded among the otherworldly shaped leaves, and the next the prickly husk of the fruit is already maturing on its broad stalk.

On a warm afternoon in the late spring of 1980, I put down the telephone receiver, turned to my wife and sighed.

"It looks like David may have found himself a girl," I said.

Bilha looked up from her magazine. "And why not? Twenty-six years old, just finished his MBA, good-looking boy from a good family. It's about time."

"Sure, sure." I gazed fondly at my wife, thinking how we had met not long after the war. We were married two years later and had had three precious children and a beautiful life. Certainly it was fitting for my son to want to share his future with someone too. And yet.

"Of course it's time," I said, settling onto the couch beside her. "It's just that with Tamar married in Chicago, Daphnae living there too, and David already so long in Boston. . . . " Why finish the sentence I didn't want to hear myself? Bilha always knew what I was thinking anyway.

But when she didn't say anything, I spoke again.

"You know I've been thinking about going back to Kazimierza Wielka. I want to take him there. He's already a manager in his company. With a wife too, he'll have so many commitments. Other things on his mind. We'll never get to go together, just the two of us." I paused. "I'll take you there someday too, of course. But this first time back, I need to go with my son. I need to show him, and them, and maybe most of all myself, that I rose from the cesspool of that goddamned war and did something good with my life."

She was silent for longer than I expected. At last she said, "Yes. It's the right thing. It's good for you to go back with David."

By the time we arranged their schedules to take two weeks off of work, found a suitable Polish tour company, purchased tickets and rendezvoused in Boston to board the Lot flight, it was already autumn. The High Holidays came early that year; we left as soon as they were over. The Polish trade union Solidarnosc had just been legalized after several years of protests and subsequent crackdowns. We read the papers regularly; the political situation in Poland was changing every day. It was a small opening in more than thirty years of Soviet repression, and I was looking forward to seeing the results firsthand. Despite everything that had happened, Poland was my native land. I cared what happened to it, even if I couldn't always say that I loved it. Even if I couldn't forgive what had happened to my family.

As for my hometown of Kazimierza Wielka, the last time I saw it I was eighteen years old, fleeing the Germans for the nearby Krakow ghetto after months in hiding. I had heard plenty of horror stories from my mother and aunt, among others, of violence against survivors who had returned too soon after the war. Just the thought that the Jews might dare to reclaim their property from their Catholic neighbors had been enough to justify violence, even murder. Add to that the fact that my father had testified against a Polish policeman in the 1960s for the killing of his aunt Frymet Rakowska, and who knew what would happen when I showed my face again in town? I had lain awake too many nights wondering how I could put himself and his son at risk of humiliation, or much worse. Oh, how my mother had begged me not to return! I knew I was a brave man; as a youth I had withstood stints in the camps, even a death march. I had saved the lives of refugee children by helping them get to Eretz Yisrael. But now I was middle-aged, and this was my own child. Then there was the trauma to Bilha and my daughters if David or I were to meet with any harm.

"Still, it was my home," I murmured, gazing out the airplane window at the cottony clouds. "I can't live in fear all my life. I can't let them do that to me."

"Huh?" David, in the aisle seat opposite, had been staring at the unappetizing-looking beef patty on his plate. A ghostly column of cigarette smoke wafted up from the rear of the plane. His side of the plane was the smoking side.

Now David looked over at me. Even if I had spoken aloud there was no guarantee he would have heard me. The seats rattled on the Soviet-made plane like teeth chattering with cold. Or with fear.

"I didn't say anything." I reached over to pat my son's arm. "I was thinking out loud."

It occurred to me, not for the first time, how perfect it was that here I had become a success in the home-building business, when my own home had been forcibly taken from his family. Had it been a subconscious choice, this career, or was it fate? Probably something much more mundane, such as that my father was in the business.

Just then, the older woman sitting by the window turned to me and asked in Polish, "Sir, do you mind if I pull down the shade?"

How long had it been since I'd heard Polish? Apart from English, I always spoke to my fellow Jewish immigrants in Yiddish, and to Bilha in Hebrew. And yet I answered without a thought.

"*Tak, oczywiście.*" Yes, of course.

She smiled broadly when she realized I was a native speaker.

"Where do you come from?" she asked, offering me a small wrapped candy from the few on her tray table.

I waved it away with a polite smile. "Near Krakow. About thirty miles northeast." I told her the name of my birthplace and was not surprised that she hadn't heard of it. "It was a small town when I was there as a boy. Just a few thousand people. Today I hear there are tens of thousands."

We talked for a few minutes about the country, about the news, about our families. When the friendly stranger settled down for a nap, I realized to my shock that my eyes were filled with tears. I, Shmuel Menachem Rakowski, age fifty-six, was headed home at last.

The tour group included South Americans and Germans, all non-Jews who were just as eager for the subsequent stops in Austria and Hungary as we were to go to Poland. They visited the major cities in the country, stopping at very few Jewish sites. Along with everyone else, David and I marveled at the restored city center in Warsaw, a UNESCO World Heritage site, and at the raw beauty of Planty, the historic green belt of Krakow, and the Jewish quarter. We went to Auschwitz, but only, as the Communists said, to honor our dead comrades. When our people were alive, I thought ruefully, we weren't comrades. We were only Jews.

It wasn't until the final day of the trip that we were able to skip the day's itinerary and carve out a window of time to visit Sam's hometown. Despite the fact that I'd been looking forward to this day with as much apprehension as excitement, I was dressed and ready to leave the Holiday Inn before David had even finished breakfast. Desperate to stem my rising dread, I leafed through the telephone book in the lobby. There it was: Smiegel, Lutek. The name of a school acquaintance. Not many people had telephones, but Lutek was a teacher. I called him and we spoke briefly, mostly exchanging memories.

And then we were on their way. The cab took us through undulating hills of pine forests and rich farmland, along the river, then toward the towering chimney of the beet sugar finery, emitting its distinctive, putrid odor. It put me in mind of Timken, how since 1901 the roller bearing company had owned Canton, eventually offering jobs in the steel industry as well, before moving production, like the car makers it served, overseas. Then we came to Krakowska Sreet, where the wooden synagogue had once stood. We passed by Sienkiewicza, with the church and the cemetery, new homes juxtaposed with old.

I cleared my throat. "My old street," I told my son. "Sienkiewicza. The only place in the world where no one has to ask me where I'm from."

Now we were moving through the market square, the smaller cobblestoned streets, the homes of Nusbaum and Ernreich and Kocerba, and Fishler, Spokoine, Pshicholsky—so much was just as I had remembered it, but then so much had also changed.

"I'd like you to stop at the railway station," I told the driver. Turning to David, I added, "There are always *kibitzers* there who will know me."

When they arrived, some of the older workers came over to chat.

"You know who lives here?" one of them said, when he recognized me. "Wojiech Guca. Remember him?"

I nodded. "Ah yes, a good man. He worked closely with my father."

"He's taken over some of your properties," another worker said. "That's not right. You should confront him."

I gave a noncommittal shrug. That wasn't why I was there.

News travels fast in a small town: Guca didn't seem overly surprised to see us pull up. When I spotted the tall, once-handsome man, now stooped and in his nineties, I wondered what the older man saw when he looked at me. Guca spread out his arms for a hug, and I came into them, but my heart was a stone.

The new brick house was far nicer than where Guca had once lived in Zagorcyze, a few kilometers away. It was well furnished, with comforts unimaginable the last time I had been in the town. Indoor plumbing. A full kitchen.

"Nice place," I said approvingly. "Tell me; how do you afford it?"

Guca didn't meet my eyes. "Brother in Canada," he muttered.

Within minutes, we were seated around the table, toasting each other with vodka in crystal glasses and eating chicken soup and goose meat.

David, whose Polish was non-existent, had been fairly silent since we'd arrived. But at the taste of the food Guca's daughter had prepared for us, he said, "Dad, this tastes just like what they serve at Yarkona!"

I nodded and translated for his hosts. Then he added, "Yarkona is where his mother comes from, in Israel," I said. Guca smiled and clapped David on the shoulder, while I put down his fork and passed around my wallet for the family to ooh and aah at the photos of my wife and daughters.

"I helped some of Shmuel's family get to Krakow in '42," Guca told David, pointing a thumb to his chest. "I helped them escape the Nazis. You're alive today because of me."

With a nod, I told David what the man had said. "It's true," I added. "You might not exist without Guca." I went on to explain that in the early days of the occupation, Guca had taken me under his personal protection to one of the areas where the family owned timber. We had walked, because Jews were no longer allowed to ride the trains.

Guca winked. "Sometimes we stayed with the forest ranger—in the same room, the same bed, even!"

I translated, and David nodded, fascinated.

"Guca," I said suddenly, "I'd like to show my son our house on Sienkiewicza."

"I'll go with you," Guca's daughter said, rising from the table. "I work there. I'm a nurse."

I wasn't sure what she meant until the taxi reached number 19 on my old street. The house where I had lived, which in my mind was still a two-storied, brown structure made of wood situated adjacent to the family lumber yard, was now, to my surprise, an upscale medical clinic. When we approached, we were met by a clutch of neighbors who were simply interested in a stranger in a taxi. To my surprise, I immediately knew all the faces, and, little by little some of the older people recognized me, and they cried out in delight, showering us with hugs and kisses. How could I stay hurt and angry, I wondered, with a welcome like this?

"Do you know who you have in your cab?" one old man leaned into the window to ask the driver. "This here is the prince of the street!"

When I translated for David, my son looked puzzled. "Why do they call you that?"

I shrugged. "God only knows."

The neighbors shook hands and marveled at David, so good-looking and healthy, so American. I translated some of their remarks. A few of them followed us into the facility, and the staff and patients looked on in amusement when I pointed out the corner where I had slept, along with everyone else's places. The workers showed off some of the remodeling since the war. There wasn't much else to do there, and I felt a curious pang of emptiness, which I quickly scotched. Better the trip be anticlimactic than too exciting, I told himself.

Before leaving town, we visited the Smiegels. Then the Krochmans at their *cukierna*, the cake shop, where they offered us coffee and ice cream.

Later we and our growing entourage strolled the cobblestone streets to the one-room house where I was born. After that, and after promising to return, we climbed into another cab to return to Krakow. On the drive, David must have noticed that I was uncharacteristically silent.

"Are you glad we came, Dad?" he asked softly. "Because I sure am. Just the thought that so many generations of our family lived here until 1942. That was really something."

I didn't answer directly. Next week at this time, I would probably be sitting in my living room watching college football. Flashes of sound and color and emotion were filling my brain. A Gypsy tune. The roar of planes overhead, and artillery on the ground. The feeling of terror. A stockade. A march.

"Hard to believe thirteen percent of the population disappeared from here, and now they act like we're beloved friends," I said. "Don't get me wrong. I'm glad they are, but still, it's hard to believe. When I think back on those years. . . ."

And then, as if time were simply a velvet curtain to be swept aside, I did.

Chapter 28

Could You Talk More About Getting Involved in Holocaust Education?

"Do I have nightmares about the war? Good question." I looked out over the heads of the students to meet the gaze of my good friend the college president. It was something we had talked about more than once, early on in our friendship.

"Some survivors I know do have nightmares about those awful days, of course. I've never had any that I know of, but I'll tell you, my sleep is still disrupted. I suffer from very bad insomnia, but not for the reasons you might think. You see, I lie awake most nights working to remember things, such as details about the barn where I hid, or what it felt like to be in such and such a situation. Then sometimes other things, like what happened when I was six, pop into my head without my even trying."

That was the main answer to the question, but there was something more I needed to say. I scratched my head. How to put this? I cleared my throat.

"Along with that, I also lie there at night trying to imagine myself in other people's places. I put myself in the shoes of people who weren't able to survive. For example, what would I have felt running from the school if, instead of being in hiding, I were one of the students when the Germans came in with their guns?"

The lecture hall was completely still. One hundred pairs of eyes tracked my every movement. One hundred pairs of ears listened to my every word. Sometimes I couldn't believe it was I who was holding them spellbound.

Until 1961, it never occurred to me to speak about my wartime experiences to anyone outside of immediate family and friends. My reasoning was simple. Years earlier, just after the war, I was talking to a Russian officer who was holding me up on my way to Krakow. When I told him that I had been interred in German camps, his answer was brutal.

"A Polish Jew in Krakow?" He gave me a nasty look. "Only one way you could have survived, kid. You must have collaborated with the Nazis. I should shoot you right here."

It didn't get any better after that. When some of the Poles saw me return to the country, they treated me as though I were one Jew too many. Even in Eretz Yisrael, some of the Jews looked down on the dead as "sheep who went willingly to the slaughter." It's not that anyone said those exact words to me, but they didn't have to. It was evident in the way they looked at us refugees, the way they talked. And Americans? They simply didn't want to hear it. Sometimes they would ask a question or two, but when I started to answer, their eyes glazed over. At that time, most Americans were either celebrating the Allied victory or suffering through the Communist witch-hunts. And most of the Jews who came up in normal conversation were those in the U.S. entertainment industry who had been blacklisted for alleged Party membership. Among my people, meanwhile, it wasn't always much better. Maybe it was their guilt at having escaped the horrors of Europe in cushy America, or of not doing more to save us. Or maybe it was the fact that so many Jews were busy celebrating the birth of our new country. It was a time to look forward to a bright new future, not the horrifying past! Maybe it was that.

Then came the trial of Adolf Eichmann, the war criminal of all war criminals, the Nazi behind the mass deportation and slaughter of European Jews known as the Final Solution. The Israelis finally tracked him down in Argentina, where he had quietly lived and worked after the war. He was arrested in May, 1960, and his trial began nearly a year later. Unlike the Nuremberg Trials soon after the war, this time the survivors were allowed more of a voice. It made all the difference. So did the television cameras that broadcast coverage all over the world. Suddenly the world's attention began to turn toward us, like flowers toward the sun.

By the time the monster was executed on June 1, 1962, I was a public speaker.

I started by talking mainly in schools. It was the logical first step, because Bilha was very active in education. I think I also figured that adults had already made up their minds about things, whereas children were still open to listening and learning. I was never a shy guy, and the more I talked, and the more questions they asked, the more comfortable I became in front of groups. After a while, it was almost as though this were what I had been born to do. Who knows? Maybe I was.

Then I met the president of Walsh College, now a university, in North Canton. The school was run by the Jesuits, and the president, who was a monk, was a good man. His name was Father Francis Blouin. Bilha attended classes there, and by and by we grew close. Francis Blouin took me all over the city to speak to adult audiences. He even published a paper based on his belief that the whole "Jews killed Jesus" belief was a straight piece of anti-Semitism with no basis in fact. Among other places, I spoke at his school, for the Catholic brotherhood, even on the radio.

I grew more and more at ease on these engagements. I was invited to Malone, the city's Quaker university. I always spoke personally, even to the chemists who were discussing the gas used in the asphyxiation process in the death camps. Then the diocese in Youngstown invited me to speak to the bishop.

Before long, I was speaking all over the place. And along with my speaking, I started to attend the big international gatherings of survivors, one in Israel in 1981, another in 1983. Like the rest of my family, I also began to make donations, to the planned Holocaust Memorial Museum in Washington, D.C., and others.

The more I spoke, the more I remembered. The more I remembered, the more I spoke. And the more I spoke, the better I felt.

Chapter 29

What Made You Go Back to Poland in 1989?

Our fortieth wedding anniversary was approaching, and I didn't know what to get Bilha. It seemed to me she had everything she wanted—books, clothing, jewelry—and what she didn't have, she could just go out and get for herself. So one night at supper, I asked her. And her response, though unusual, didn't surprise me a bit.

"There's only one thing I really want," she said, almost before I'd gotten the question out. It was as though she had been waiting for me to ask, which, come to think of it, she probably had. "I want to go to Poland. I want to see Kazimierza Wielka, and all the places you went before and during the war, and all the places you weren't, but that I've read about in these books." She gestured toward the dozens of volumes about the Holocaust and Polish Jewry she'd been collecting and reading for years. "I need to find out what the people remember of their Jewish neighbors, their culture, their homes. I need to see what if anything is left there of Jewish life."

I understood why. Not only was she the wife of a survivor, but Bilha well knew from all her reading that before the war, Polish Jews had made up the primary Jewish diaspora, with a culture that had evolved over nearly a thousand years. The destruction of this once-vibrant people was for her, a Jew and a student of history, nearly as soul-crushing as it had been for me. It made sense that she had to see it with her own eyes.

First, we went to Israel, back to Moshav Yarkona, to see Bilha's family. After our usual wonderful trip, it was strange, kissing her eighty-seven-year-old father good-bye, leaving behind the orange, pecan, and avocado groves of Israel for the narrow streets of the Old World, when so many, myself included, had risked our lives to travel in the opposite direction. But so much had changed since the war started fifty years earlier. Including us. This time, I was sixty-five years old, a grandfather and a prosperous businessman. This time, I had nothing to fear.

We arrived in Warsaw on the afternoon of September 23 and checked into the Hotel Forum. I realized as I was talking to the clerk at the front desk that in all these years, Bilha had never heard me speak Polish, although it was of course my native tongue. She didn't know the language at all.

From the hotel, we hired a guide to tour the city, which didn't have any special meaning for me apart from the history. Not that I minded. The strange thing was, so much had happened to the Jews there, but apart from a few monuments, there was so little left to see.

"In my village in Israel," Bilha told the woman, "we have signs of civilization going back three thousand years. But here, there's virtually no sign of what happened fifty years ago. It's really astonishing."

In the small Jewish Archives in the middle of the city, I was able to find information about what had gone on during the war in my town, including eyewitness reports of two shootings, one of seventeen people, the other of two or three hundred. We were both moved to see my mother's signature when she registered in Krakow after liberation, and I told her how seeing that signature had been a lifeline for me. But as for living Jews, there were just a few elderly beggars, a synagogue or cemetery caretaker or two, and no one else. You know the expression, "The silence was deafening"? Well in this case, the absence was breathtaking.

On our third night in the city, we met a distant relation of Bilha's named Maria Drewnowska, who was the wife of a prominent judge. Maria was a fascinating woman. She and I talking about the current situation in Poland for several hours, and I got a good sense of what was going on. I felt sorry for Bilha that because they had no common language, they couldn't communicate directly, but I did my best to interpret.

After Warsaw, we traveled through the countrywide to the death camp of Treblinka, where some of my neighbors and relatives were among the 800,000 who were murdered. One of my cousins, Sruel Rakowski, helped lead the rebellion there. It was strange to be driving toward this hellish place on such a beautiful fall day. When we arrived, it was even stranger. Once again, there was little at the site of the camp besides the railroad tracks and a small museum.

"This is the end of the world," the driver said, as we trod through the soft, ashen dirt beneath our feet. I knew it to be true, and yet with the birds singing and my wife by my side it was so hard to believe. We signed our names in the museum guest book after scanning the heartbreaking comments in Hebrew, English, and other languages. Then we stood by the monument and said Kaddish. We were deeply touched, and all around us, tears were flowing. Two weeping Polish women seemed to want to talk to us, but I quickly turned away. When at last we returned to Warsaw that evening, all I wanted to do was sleep. Thankfully, Bilha understood. After the emotional day, she seemed to need the same.

After that, I decided to serve as my own guide, and Bilha gladly agreed. We rented a little red Renault, bought a map and headed for Radom. I could see that this city had done well for itself over the years, and the Jewish section was intact, albeit devoid of Jews. From there we went looking for Pionki, the nearby town with the camp in which I had spent that terrible year in the ammunition factory. Amazingly, we came across a young man who worked in the same factory where I had, and he directed us right to it. I could feel the anticipation rising in my chest as the factory gates came into view. It was not exactly a homecoming, but I was anxious to find some closure.

At the entrance, we were directed to the commander in charge. It seemed that the place now manufactured bombs and missiles, so it was run by the military.

"I request permission to tour the factory," I said, with as much politeness as I could muster. "I was an inmate here forty-six years ago. I worked as a slave laborer."

The officer looked at me in disbelief. Or was it disgust?

"You can't come in here!" he thundered. "This is the most secret factory in Poland!" As he talked, other officers gathered, clearly looking for a little entertainment.

"At least may I see the camp where I suffered and so many of my friends died?"

The man raises his eyebrows. "Only Jews were in that camp." At the word *Yudas*, or Jews, he made the gesture of a beard.

"I am a Jew," I said. "Do I have a beard?"

For several seconds the officers looked from me to each other, clearly astonished. At last they began to laugh. Finally one of them said, "We'll give you a room, a meal, even a woman." Here he winked a little crudely at Bilha. "But you can't go into this factory. It's strictly forbidden."

There was nothing I could do. I was angry, but I couldn't show it. It seemed I was as powerless in this place today as I had been half a century earlier. Except, of course, that this time, I had an automobile to leave in instead of a cattle car. That fact—and my wife beside me—calmed me like nothing else could have. We walked back to the Renault, and in the rearview mirror I saw the officers watch us drive off. And that was the end of that.

We then headed to the labor camp in Skarzysko-Kamienna, where my mother and Aunt Mina had been interred in 1943. We asked a young man in the town where the Jewish district was, and he offered to climb into the car to direct us.

"During the war my family hid a Jew," he told us. "We called him Uncle Moshe. He survived and became almost one of the family." When we reached the monument, we got out of the car and wandered around the place a little before heading on to Kielce.

Most of the Jewish community of Kielce had died in Treblinka or Buchenwald. The few who survived were killed in a pogrom when they tried to resume their lives. Everywhere we went we saw signs of the erasure of the Jews: nail holes in doorposts where mezuzahs once sat, buildings still bearing the faded letters of old Jewish signs. We spotted menorahs in a shop window, and when we asked about them, the proprietor told us curtly that they were candleholders. When I asked for directions to the synagogue, a woman shouted at me, "No synagogues in this town. Go to another town!"

We walked around the haunted streets, then we asked our elderly hotel concierge where the survivors had been killed. He directed us to a spot by the river. We couldn't get out of there fast enough.

"We are coming to the Jewish state now," I told Bilha, as we approached towns with once-thriving Jewish majorities. We drive through Zagrody and on to Jedrzejow, where my uncle had owned an estate. Everywhere we went we were taken with the lush landscape, the fertile fields. For the people who live here now, we knew, this is the polar opposite of the land of ghosts it has become for me.

As soon as we stopped, we drew a crowd, what with our odd car and our even odder questions. It didn't help that we were strangers in a small town that saw few visitors. One person sent us on to the next for directions, but no one gave us so much as a smile or a kind word. Once more, we were happy to leave.

Out on the road once more, we saw an old man and a young child on a tractor, plowing a field of sugar beets. I stopped the car and got out.

"Excuse me," I called out in Polish when the man cut the engine. "Can you tell me the way to Liscin?"

"Licsin?" He raised his eyebrows in surprise. "Why do you want to know? Who are you visiting there?"

"I am a Rakowski," I said proudly. "My family lived here before the war."

The man stared, as though he were seeing an apparition. Turned out he may have thought he was. He jumped off the tractor, but he didn't come any closer.

"No way!" he called out. "It can't be. I knew them all, Moniek and Srulik and all the others. They're all dead. Killed in the war, in Treblinka. Every last one of them."

"I know they were," I said, walking toward him. "But I am from Kazimierza Wielka. I am Srulik's nephew."

While he digested this information, I handed the farmer a bottle of vodka and a chocolate bar for the child. Then they joined us in the car and traveled with us the mile to where the nobleman's estate had stood.

On the way, I could barely contain my curiosity. After all, who knew how long he would talk to us?

"What happened to the estate?" I asked.

"When the Germans came," he said, "they brought a Pole from Poznan to supervise the property and flour mill. The cursed Nazis destroyed the great house. Then the Russians came when the war was over. They installed a new commissar here and divided up the estate."

All at once he told me to stop the car. "Here." He pointed to a stand of trees. "Here was where the house was. Now, it's just acacia trees." Bilha and I gazed out at the red rooster sitting on a pile of debris. He was the current master of the once-magnificent property.

"I worked for them as a blacksmith," the farmer said, perhaps to break the sad silence. "They were very good people. It's a tragedy what happened to them. But war is war."

We went with him to his house for a while, and then we took our leave. I can't say I felt good, but I was glad that people in this area would know that the Rakowskis were still alive, somewhere, and that the people who had been here would be remembered.

We next stopped in Dzialoszyce, not far from my home, where I had known some Jews. Now, it was practically deserted. An old Polish woman approached us at the synagogue and wept as she cursed the Poles who had destroyed the Jewish community there. Before we left, I handed her a little money, and she kissed our faces and hands.

From there, we drove past Skalmish, the small village where my father had owned some lumber tracts and had done a lot of business. We didn't stop. We were just six miles from my hometown. And before we got there, we had one more important visit to make.

Chapter 30

How Was It Reuniting with the Man Whose Family Hid You during the War?

After asking for directions, we came at last to the farmhouse belonging to Mietek, the son of the district representative who had helped us survive the beginning of the war, when the Germans were rounding up the Jews in Kazimierza Wielka.

"Is Mietek at home?" I asked the older woman who answered the door. I figured it must be his wife.

She crossed her arms across her aproned chest. "Why do you want to see him?"

I knew these people, and I well understood their suspicion. Strangers, especially well-dressed strangers, often meant trouble.

With a big smile I said, "To thank him for doing something he did for me a long time ago."

At these words, the woman's hard expression melted, and her eyes danced. I couldn't imagine that she knew who I was, but good news is good news.

Still staring at me, she called out over her shoulder, "Mietek, hurry, come here!"

When he came to the door, I saw at once the resemblance to his father Mleko. It was almost surreal, standing in this familiar place looking at this old man. I told him who I was.

How can I describe the look on his face, or the feelings that passed between us, when we two grandfathers laid eyes on each other for the first time in fifty years? The couple immediately invited us in for tea, and then Mietek took us on a tour of some of the places we had heard about, where so many of my neighbors had been shot and buried.

Standing in the midst of a thriving sugar beet field, he said, "One of your teenaged cousins tried to run away, and she actually got to that little brick factory not far from here. The policemen sicked their dogs on her and brought her back to be shot with the rest of the family."

While he stood by, Bilha and I said Kaddish, as we had done wherever we had traveled where Jews had been killed. Then we moved on toward the forest. A small stone monument read, "Here were killed and buried three hundred of Kazimierza Wielka's Jewish citizens by the Nazi barbarians in September, 1942." At the foot of the stone was a plaque stating that it was erected by a Meller of Winnipeg in 1987, in memory of his parents and sister who had died there.

Mietek began, slowly at first, to tell us the story of what had happened to the Jews of our town, including the man who ran off from the execution site and disappeared into the woods, leaving his wife and children behind. He ended with curses on the Nazis and the Polish collaborators.

"Israel Leveinstein is still alive and lives in a place in America called Jersey City," I told him. "In fact, one of the policemen responsible for the massacre was convicted and punished thanks to my father."

"Really? How was that?"

"He was a witness to his trial. He gave a deposition that helped proved that the man murdered members of our family."

We stood in silence. Then we returned to Mietek's house, where his wife had prepared a fine Polish dinner for us. During the meal, Bilha turned to me and told me in English to explain to Mietek about the man who took away our possessions after my father and I went through the hole in the Krakow ghetto.

After I told him, he said, "Such a barbarian. So many normal people lost the face of a human being in those crazy days. So many behaved like that! Do you know he still walks the streets of this village? We should take him and punish him. But that is a lost cause!"

I told Bilha what he said. Instead of being disappointed, she replied, "I still feel the satisfaction that some justice is being done, if only by telling this story to a good local man."

From there, it was a short trip to the farm of Mietek's cousin, where my family had stayed after leaving his father's home. Tadek, who had been ten at the time and was now a grandfather like me, opened the front door of the farmhouse to find out who we were. When I told him, his tanned and lined face lit up, and his voice grew more and more animated as he spoke.

"I was only a kid then, of course," he said, "but I remember the Jews who lived with the pigs and came out of the holes at night—and even played cards with my father! I was told not to tell anyone about you." He shook his head. "You mean you came all the way just to visit me! I can't believe it!"

His wife looked at his hands and clicked her tongue. "He's just come in from the field," she said apologetically. "If we'd known you were coming he could have cleaned up for you."

I shrugged it off, but Bilha wanted to know what she'd said. When I told her, she told me to say, "Your hands are very clean. Anyone who risked his life to save a human being has hands that are always clean." They liked that, of course. Then she asked me to tell them the story of the thirty-six *tzadikim*, the righteous people who, according to Jewish mysticism, arise in every generation to sustain the world.

"That's you," she told me to say to Mietek. "You are one of the tzadikim."

"We suffered for being good to the Jews," he told us by way of reply. "Both from the Germans and then the Communists. Life is very hard for us here." We didn't know how to respond, so he continued. "Those were terrible days. There was death on every corner. This land is soaked with the blood of suffering people. Many, many people were killed here."

As we were leaving, he asked me one last question. "How in the world did you find Mietek? You were so young then yourself."

"Not so hard," I said. "The Americans have an expression, 'a needle in a haystack.' He was easier to find than that. I remembered Mietek's father was head of the county council, and also that when I knew him he was a little hunchbacked. So I asked the local farmers if they remembered such a man, and if they knew where his family was. They discussed it among themselves, and here we are."

At last it was time to leave. Again I had the sense, as I'd had in Pionki, that the last time I left this place I'd been at the mercy of outside forces. This time, I was able to leave them with gifts and money, which they accepted gratefully. Bilha and I hugged and kissed them as though we were family. And then it was time to take my wife to my town.

Chapter 31

How Did You Feel Going Back to Kazimierza Wielka the Second Time?

Not so much had changed from when I was in my hometown with David nine years earlier, but now, I was better prepared, at least emotionally. For Bilha, who had heard my stories for most of her life, it was nothing short of a revelation. She was all eyes and ears as I took her from street to street, to the market, to the home of the anti-Semite Kocerba, or of my family and friends. I was glad that it was a beautiful day, with a few buoyant clouds scattered in a crystal blue sky. As always during harvest season, the odor of sugar beets was so intense not only you could taste it, you could practically see it.

I had had no agenda for the visit other than to show Bilha around, but now, suddenly, I had an idea. "You see that house over there?" I pointed to a building larger than some of the others around it. A man I didn't know was working out front.

"The mayor used to live there," I told her. "Pshicholsky. He was a good man, who hid my aunt for a long time. And his daughter, Sofia, was in my class. She was a really fine girl. I'll bet she still lives here. Let's pay her a visit." My smiling wife gave an enthusiastic nod.

"Hello!" I called out in Polish as we approached. "Does Sofia live here? Is she home?"

He stared at me, then his eyes lit up. "Hey, I remember you! Rakowski!" Without waiting for my reply, he called back into the open door of the house. "Sofia! Come here!"

The plump, gray-haired woman who emerged moments later let out a yelp of delight.

"Shmulik, my friend, my friend!" After a quick hug and an invitation inside, she rushed into the kitchen. Over coffee and dessert, we talked about all the shared history between us, as well as those things I didn't already know. I didn't know my aunt had lived in the basement. Or what happened to the Fishlers, the Rozanecks, the Zalmans and others. When we'd gotten through the subject of my family's war—so much sadness, so much death—they told us about their own son, living in Pennsylvania with his wife and two children.

We left town soon after, and drove the short distance to pay our respects at Auschwitz, then on to Krakow. Neither Bilha nor I have ever said Kaddish so often in such a short time. Then we returned to Kazimierza Wielka. This time Sofia was making noodles, and we sat down to a large meal of hot borscht and veal, cabbage and cooked beets. Afterward we marveled over old photographs, and Sofia's husband Jerzek, who'd asked around a little while we were gone, informed us of the fate of more family and friends. He told us that my grandmother, shot by the Germans when we couldn't take her with us into hiding, was buried in a Christian cemetery. Over the years, others were buried on top of her.

Was it that story when it started, when I began to lose it, when this reunion was no longer simply riveting, but more deeply disturbing? I could feel Bilha's eyes on me as my face began to grow hot. She knew me so well.

But not Jerzek. At one point he said, "Hey, do you remember the Brandenburg brothers from Odonov? Meyer and Baruch? They were very good friends of mine. Gifted students. They went into hiding in the brick factory. We all tried to look out for them, but one day, not long before the end of the war, someone reported them to the police. We never heard from them again."

"Not to worry," I told him. "They're both doing well in New York."

When Jerzek heard that, he called out the news to Sofia, who at that point was busy washing dishes. Then he told me there was still one Jew in town, Mathi Singer. I knew his nephew in Canton. Mathi, he told me, married a Polish woman and was doing well.

"Do you remember the butcher's son, Shmulik?" Jerzek asked suddenly. "He survived in the forest, carrying a butcher's knife in his boot. Then just before Liberation, he disappeared, too."

Story after story went on like that until I couldn't take it anymore. I tried to hold back the fury rising inside me, but it was like redirecting a tidal wave.

Holding up my hand I said, "You know something? There's a big problem between the Jews and the Poles. We really have a bitter score to settle. You tell me how hard it was to keep the Jews alive, and I understand that. But tell me something: If people cared so much, why are the few monuments Jews have paid to put up in such bad shape?" As I began to speak, I heard my voice grow hoarse with emotion. "Not to mention those you call traitors and collaborators, even the AK (Armia Krajowa), your heroes, who tracked down Jews. And why did the Poles attack and even kill so many of us who came back after to survive?" I thought of my aunt who broke her leg escaping from the house. "Look how many years it took me to come back!"

Sofia came out from the kitchen, drying her hands. "You're right, but please remember something, Shmulik. There are many good Poles who did their best." She went on for a while in this way, speaking softly about how now the Polish pope and the local priest teach them that all men are brothers. Finally I interrupted her.

"The Jews are still blamed for everything, including Communism and poverty!" I could feel the atmosphere had grown tense. Part of me wanted to stop, but another part of me didn't. These feelings had been festering for too long, like a deep wound that just won't heal. Exactly like a wound.

We talked some more, each side failing to completely capture the feelings of the other. Finally we left the house to say Kaddish at the Jewish monuments. We laid flowers at the stones, at the site of the old synagogue, where no holy books or objects remained, and at the field where seventeen people had been shot and buried.

It was time to go. The mood lifted somewhat as we gave them the gifts we had brought. Just as Bilha and I were getting into the car, I turned to Jerzek.

"Just tell me. Did anyone at all of my family survive?"

He shook his head. "I don't know. Go to see Guca and ask him about your cousin Roseneck. He may know where she is now."

On our way out of town we stopped at my old school. The principal was helpful, showing me my old school records. I was happy to show my wife the educator how well I'd done! The principal proudly told us that the current students know that the school was turned into a labor camp for 300 Jews in 1942, and that two weeks later the people there were killed.

"Do you show them the monument in the woods, or the location of the synagogue?" I ask.

She didn't answer, and that was answer enough.

After a nice reunion with an old teacher of mine, we went over to Guca's house. His home was more elegant than any I'd seen. When I mentioned it, he explained again that any wealth he had was thanks to his brother in Chicago, who had left him a lot of money when he passed away.

"What happened to the properties you owned with my father?" I asked, as casually as I could.

All he said was, "The Germans took them." What was I going to do? There was no way I could ask for any of our lands back. Thankfully, I didn't need it. Not only had I done well for myself in America, but my father had also received money for the house from the U.S. Treasury for Polish Assets. In addition my parents both got monthly reparations from the German government, and even I got a little. I was more interested in information.

"What happened to my cousin Rosenka? I heard you might know."

"Let it go, Shmulik. It's old history. Everybody's gone."

I couldn't do that so easily, of course. "Tell me, what do you know?"

He shook his head. "I heard she married a Pole and moved away."

"But where?"

His daughter Vera, a beautiful woman in her fifties, cleared her throat. "Please, Mr. Rakowski. Let it go. They're all dead now."

I didn't respond to her. Instead, I asked Guca to call his granddaughter into the room. She was a twenty-one-year-old student of history at Krakow University.

Seconds later she stood before me, looking as fresh and innocent as a lamb. "Young lady," I asked her, "have you ever seen a Jew before today?"

She looked at me, then at her mother, then back to me. "I don't know."

"Do we look any different from your parents, or anybody else?" She stared. I continued. "Do you know what a synagogue is?"

"I've never heard that word."

I turned to her mother. "Vera, do you know where the synagogue was? Third block from your house, that empty lot with big holes in the ground."

"Oh? I saw the ruins of one in Dzialoszyce one time."

Now there was another conversation about how hard it was to help the Jews, how more than once Guca was lucky to escape with his life.

"Janina," I asked the young girl at one point. "Tell me, did you learn in school what happened to the Jews of Poland?"

She bit her lip. "We've only reached the fourteenth century."

We enjoyed more fine Polish food from our hosts, we had more gifts to give them, and then we took our leave. But I couldn't get Rosenka out of my mind. Could they be protecting her new identity? I felt so helpless, not knowing if they were holding something back from me.

We made one more visit, to the Molenda family that had lived next to our lumberyard. The brick house was two stories high. Molenda's daughter welcomed us, and Bilha spoke a little English with her husband while we drank tea. In between sips I looked around the living room, peering at each object as though I were in a museum. I couldn't help it. Where was our furniture, our ornaments, our books? Who had them?

She knew what I was doing, of course. "The police took everything, from both your house and ours," she said bluntly.

We talked about mutual friends, including my Aunt Frania, who she said had wandered from place to place after leaving her hiding spot in town. Like a hunted criminal. Like an animal.

"Many times at night she used to knock at my back door. The signal was three knocks. I would recognize it was her and put out some food."

When I told her that Aunt Frania had not survived the war, she shook her head.

At last I had had enough. We said our good-byes, left town, and went on to Krakow. From there we traveled to Berlin and Sachsenhausen, where I found my bunk in barrack 38.

By then I was ready to go home. I mean Canton. It's true that Kazimierza Wielka is the only place I could ever go where people don't have to ask me where I'm from. They know. I am, after all, a Rakowski. But it hadn't been home for a long time.

I needed to go home to America.

Chapter 32

What Was Your Experience with March of the Living?

> God, full of compassion, on high, provide a sure rest on the wings of the Divine, within the purview of the holy, pure and glorious, whose shining is like that of the sky, to the soul of this man, son of his father, for charity given to the memory of his soul. Thus the Master of Compassion will protect him forever, from behind his wings, and will tie his soul with the bonds of life.
>
> (Jewish prayer *Al Maaleh Rahamim*)

"It was such a cool honor being in Poland with you this week, Sam. I'm never gonna forget you. And ya know what? I'm gonna share your story and teach people about anti-Semitism for the rest of my life."

We were seated on long, low padded benches in a spare Polish hotel lobby, awaiting our bus to the airport. Not two minutes before, the young people had been giggling and horsing around. Now they were all looking at me, deadly serious. Even after a week with them, and several meetings before leaving the States, I was still taken a little aback at these alternating flashes of youth and maturity. I was just opening my mouth to respond to the tall high school senior when another young girl cut in.

"Sam! I can't believe I got to spend this whole entire week with you! You know my sister's talked about you for years, ever since her own Poland trip! We love you! You are such a hero!"

A number of the kids cheered and clapped me—gently, as if I were a porcelain teacup—on the back. Happy as I was, I was beginning to wonder if I would ever get a word in edgewise.

"Please, *chevrei*," I said, using the Hebrew word for "friends" that the kids knew from youth groups and day schools. "A hero I'm not. Maybe those who died were heroes, but I was just lucky. Okay, determined. But no braver than others. Mostly very, very lucky."

"Well you're a hero for telling your story!" someone called out. I didn't know who it was. After a while the sea of smiling young Jewish faces, healthy and rosy-cheeked under red, blonde and mostly brown hair, ran together. They were the Jewish future, and from where I stood, it looked astonishing.

The first time I went with the March of the Living program to tell my story in Poland was in 1995. Here's how it happened. One evening after work, I was sitting at home in Canton reading the paper on the couch when the phone rang.

"Hello, Sam?" The Israeli voice on the other end was familiar, but I wasn't sure.

"Fisher, is that you?"

"Yeah, how you doing, Sam? You good? The family good?"

This Fisher was the head of B'nai B'rith International, the renowned Jewish service organization. He was a busy man who did not call for nothing. And I myself had had a long day.

"Yeah, yeah, we're good. What can I do for you?"

"Sam, I need you to go on March of the Living. You know what is March of the Living?"

I knew, more or less, although now of course I know much more. It's an annual educational program founded by two Israelis in 1988. They take high school students on a tour of Jewish cultural and historical sites in Poland—including a March of the Living, as opposed to a Death March—from Auschwitz to Birkenau camps on *Yom Hashoa*, Holocaust Remembrance Day. Most then go on to Israel for a second week to commemorate Yom Hazikaron, Israel's Remembrance Day, and *Yom Ha'atzmaut*, Israel's Independence Day. I knew a few survivors who had gone, or who had been interested in going, to tell their stories to the kids.

"Yes, sure I know. And it sounds good. But when is the trip?"

He told me the dates, and I shook my head. Then I realized he couldn't see me on the phone.

"Sorry, Fisher. Not this year. Bilha and I have a trip to China on April 30. I'd be glad to go back to Poland with the kids. But I can't do the Israel part."

"That's fine. Thanks, Sam. I'll send you all the information. We'll meet in the hotel in Baltimore the day before the trip, because we're flying out of there."

I didn't think much more about it until the package of material arrived a few days later. Then I started to get excited. I saw that I would be telling my story to thirty high school juniors and seniors from B'nai B'rith's youth organization. That among other places of interest, like the Warsaw Ghetto and important mass graves, we would be going to the city of Radom, where some of my friends had come from.

One evening, I was looking over the brochure at the kitchen table when I noticed Bilha leaning over my shoulder.

"What do you think?" I asked, my eyes still on the photos of smiling children, their arms interlocked with those of survivors.

"I think I want to come with you." She dropped into the chair next to mine.

I looked at her. "You've been with me to Poland already."

"Sure, but not like this. I'm an educator, Sam. This is a wonderful educational experience. Something really special."

I could see how interested she was. And she was right; she would get a lot from the trip. She would bring a lot to the kids. Still, I had to be honest with her.

"I don't think so."

She frowned. "Why not? You know I wouldn't get in the way."

"Of course you would. Not intentionally, but you would. If I am with my wife, as I will be in China a week later, by the way, I will be thinking of my wife. I will be talking with my wife. I will be responsible for my wife. This is a trip I have to make by myself. I have to be there for them."

What did I mean by them, exactly? The students? The organizers? The other survivors? Or the dead I was going to attempt to resurrect with my stories? I didn't know. I just knew I had to do this alone.

As always, Bilha understood. She was disappointed, but she understood. Since then, each year after I attend, we sit together and watch the five-hour video of the trip.

After a couple of meetings and phone calls, I arrived at the hotel in Baltimore. Sitting in the lobby were the two people I knew from Radom, whom I'd spent time with in a couple of camps. We embraced and chatted like any old friends. No casual onlooker could have imagined what we'd shared.

I've been asked if the tour upset me, and all I can say is, it was the total opposite. I had no problem at all. When I talked to the kids, they were very impressed. They liked me, I think, because I let them be themselves. Some of them were really on edge about their reactions. We were touring Auschwitz when somebody made a nervous joke in my hearing. I turned around to see, and when we made eye contact, all the blood drained from the poor boy's face.

"Don't worry!" I said, loud enough so that the others could hear. "You know by now that I make plenty of jokes myself. When I was in Berlin just before the fall of the Wall, I told a Congressman I was with that I wasn't so happy about reunification. After all, I said, that was the wall of their own camp! And when I saw the Germans with their dogs at the Reichstag, I said, 'What a wonderful site! They set the dogs on themselves!'"

I was glad to see that a few of the kids chuckled.

"What I'm saying is, you can laugh; you can say what you want. All I ask is that you listen and learn. If you listen, I will be happy. That's why I'm here."

Something shifted after that. The children loosened up before my eyes. At least they did with me. I don't know about the other survivors.

That afternoon, we were walking around the monument to Mila 18 in Warsaw. I was talking to the kids about the Polish Resistance when I noticed that another group was inching forward to hear. Then they asked me some questions. I found out later they were from Cincinnati, and they had no survivors with them.

Not all of the survivors took to it like I did. After all, everybody's different. And some people are more damaged, or less educated, or naturally more shy. I tried to take care of them, to show them how it's done. I think I was effective not only because I had the knowledge, but also I was able to be more positive. I didn't tell a lot of terrible stories. I was trying to teach the children how I felt. What it felt like to be in a cattle car, what it felt like to move from one place to another, to be hungry for eight months. I didn't tell them every single detail, but what I told them, both the details and the emotions, I was very honest about. And because of that, people trusted me.

It also helped that I speak Polish, Hebrew, Yiddish and English. The guides and security people were Polish in Poland and Israeli in Israel, so I could communicate with them. We got along very well. The Poles in particular had so many questions, were so hungry for education about the history.

I loved that program. Every year I worked hard, but I also paid my own expenses. They paid hotels and food, airfare, but I made donations to them over the years. I believed in what they were doing. I only had a problem with one thing. The organizers had the group say Kaddish, the Jewish prayer for the dead, in front of a mass grave. I couldn't do it. Throughout the familiar prayer, which I've said a thousand times, I stayed silent.

Afterward, several of the kids came over to me.

"Sam?" one girl asked. That surprised me; she was usually very quiet, especially in front of others. "We didn't see your lips move. How come you didn't say Kaddish?"

I shook my head. "I'm not sure I'm comfortable praising God at a spot where four thousand people have died. Next time, maybe I can lead you in another prayer."

After that, I spoke to the leader. And the next time, I led another prayer typically said over the dead. It's called "*El Maleh Rachamim*. God Is Full of Compassion."

I continued participating in the March after moving to Florida, Altogether, I've gone eleven times. Over the years, of course, fewer survivors accompanied me. The March changed in other ways, too. For one thing, because I was more experienced, my talks improved. And the groups got larger. One time I gave a pep talk to about 140 kids about how to face the music when they went to college and talked to Palestinians. I told them about advocating for the Jewish people, how they mustn't give up. And I got so many notes from the young people, whether in the little notebooks they gave us to fill with impressions from the trip or in actual letters. One girl from New Zealand told me she became more Jewish because of me. Another young girl had told me during a pre-trip meeting that she was going with a non-Jewish boyfriend. Not three days into the trip she came up to me, gave me a hug, and said, "Sam, I've decided I'm going to marry Jewish." And one year we had a huge reunion at our house. I've never seen anything like it. The *nachas* of a wedding with the *mishigas* of a bar mitzvah!

In the spring of 2016, I attended a pre-trip meeting with the kids at the Donna Klein Day School with my arm in a sling.

"Sam! What happened?" Everybody, teachers and students both, looked at me in concern.

I shrugged. "Nothing much. We're moving into our new place, and I slid on some newspapers on the floor. Me, all I got was a broken arm."

"But we're leaving for Poland tomorrow!"

"That's not the worst of it! I can't help my wife unpack!"

Wouldn't you know that some of the kids, under the supervision of one of the mothers, who happened to be an interior decorator, unpacked us and set up the whole place?

There were so many experiences like this, more than I can count. But the absolute high point of the trips for me was 2015, when my family from New Jersey joined me on the March. It was a big decision for the organizers, because they had to change the route for me. But they did it. My cousin Rella and her children accompanied me to my family house in Kazimierza Wielka, along with 140 kids. I gave a speech right in front of it. The mayor came to greet us, but really the whole town was involved, including, of course, the Polish families who had hidden us. It had a big effect, all those young people in their March of the Living jackets, walking through town. Afterward, the kids presented me with a picture of the Superman logo.

2019 was the last year I attended the March. Of course it was canceled in 2020 due to the pandemic, but that wasn't the reason. Now I'm ready and willing, but the organization can't insure me anymore. I'm too old. This year, 2022, they do not expect to have any survivors on the trip. That is the way of the world. That is why it was so urgent for those children to listen when they could.

Chapter 33

What Have You Done Recently to Educate the Public About the Holocaust?

"When I walked out of those woods there, I became a survivor."

All these years I've been teaching about the Shoah, but in 2021 and 2022 I've really been very much in demand. Of course I know why. There are so few of us still around. Friends of mine who were very active are either not well enough to speak publicly or are no longer alive.

In late 2021, two people came to my apartment to videotape me for the Holocaust Memorial Museum in Washington D.C. I have been very active with the museum. Many of my family members and I were founders, and over the years I've given the Museum photos, artifacts and cash donations.

These two who came were fairly young. I know it was their job, but still, it's always so good to see young people interested in this history. After the young man set up all kinds of recording equipment, his partner began her questions.

"Where were you born?"

I looked at this young woman sitting across from me in my home office. She was attractive, with long dark hair. She was looking at me now, but moments earlier she had been gazing in awe at the wall of pre-war photos behind me. I took a breath, settled back on the couch, and, as I've done so many times before, I began my story.

Two hours later, they had enough for the five-minute video to be shown at a dinner here in Florida to honor survivors. I told them I planned to be there to see it.

A few months later, it was coming on January 27, International Holocaust Remembrance Day. At the event at the Museum in Washington the evening before the big day, they used snippets of my video, along with those of others.

Then the Holocaust education coordinator for the county, with whom I've worked in the past, came to my apartment to photograph me lighting a candle. It was for part of an event they were doing for high school students.

After that one of the local TV stations called the building management to ask if I would like to be interviewed for their news show. We talked on Zoom for half an hour. It didn't seem like anything out of the ordinary to me, just one of hundreds of interviews I've done over the years. But apparently this was no ordinary interview for the journalist, and what she did surprised me no end. After it was over, the young woman called her competitor at another local news station and said, "You need to interview a survivor? You should talk to Sam Ron. He's really good." Now I ask you: Did Macy's ever tell Gimbels what it was doing? Who ever heard of such a thing!

But I'm so glad it happened. In walked this fragile-looking woman in a red dress.

"We're not going to take much of your time," she said, first thing. "We've got a lot of material about you already. We just want something new on tape. We'll be out of your hair before you know it."

I shrugged. It made no difference to me. As I do with everyone who comes for an interview, I showed her and her photographer the old family photos on the wall.

"These spots here, you see?" Bilha asked them, pointing to a photo of me as a young teenager.

The two leaned closer to the frame, then looked back at us. "Yeah, what is that?" the man asked. "Oil or something? Ink?"

Bilha shook her head. "It's blood. Sam's mother carried his picture in her shoe when she was in the camp."

I don't know at what point in the next half hour the woman's face began to fall, or when her voice started to quaver. As I answered her questions—far more than five minutes' worth—I saw that she was becoming more and more emotional. In all these years, I've never seen an interviewer react so strongly.

Bilha saw it, too. Always one to look out for me, she said as they were leaving, "You know, with so many people coming to interview Sam, no one has ever given him a photo, or so much as a thank-you note." They shook their heads, thanked us profusely, and were off.

I looked at the clock. It was nearly time to go to the dining room for dinner.

"What a day!" my wife said with a sigh. "I'm exhausted! All these people in and out, all this *balagan*!"

I understood. And I didn't have to say a word in response, because she knew, after seventy-two years, exactly how I felt. Of course I was worn out too. I'm ninety-eight, after all. And this kind of thing goes on day in and day out, the emails from my *shtetl* that have to be answered, or from students in Florida, or from my relatives. The telephone calls and interviews and Zoom meetings. It's exciting for both of us, being so much in demand. Being so busy with all these wonderful things, young people, TV, Washington. But of the two of us, I am the one who is more cheerful about it. Bilha is proud of me, of course, and she supports everything I do one hundred percent. After all, she is the professional educator. But it all makes me so happy. I get so much positive energy from doing these things. I honestly think that's why I survived. Like my father, I have always been positive.

We were silent for a long time, Then Bilha shifted a little in her chair.

"I think she likes you, that last one," she said.

My mind was on other things. "Who?"

"That young girl in the pretty dress. The last one. I think she really likes you."

"Oh that girl?" I laughed. "I think she loves me."

The following week, we were delighted to receive cards and photos from the people who interviewed us on this Holocaust Remembrance Day. We were delighted, yes. But we weren't a bit surprised.

Chapter 34

What Is Your Relationship Now with Your Hometown?

The entire world is a very narrow bridge
and the main thing is not to be afraid at all

—Rav Nahman of Breslov (1772–1810)

I don't want to whitewash things. I've been back to my hometown several times over the years, and not every encounter was pleasant. There was the time I visited the Soda family to insist that they tell me the truth about the deaths of my aunt and uncle Dula and their three kids, who hid in their barn for eighteen months during the war. After much hesitation, they finally directed me to the area in the yard where the bones were stuffed after the five of them were shot. I got down on my knees in the dirt and dug up every one. Then I took them with me back to Canton and reburied them in my mother's grave.

On another visit I was angry with my old classmate Sofia for refusing to tell me details about the fates of other family members. At last she said to me, "Okay, I know where your family was."

Together we went to the Mandetski house by the flourmill, opened up the table that used to belong to my parents, and over vodka I gathered more information about where my loved ones were murdered.

So my experiences with my town after the war weren't all rosy, but many of them have been pretty beautiful. In one of the most memorable moments of my 2015 March of the Living visit to Kazimierza Wielka, for example, the children in the town sang for our group an old Hasidic tune, in Polish and Hebrew. With words written by the revered Rav Nahman of Breslov, born 250 years ago in Ukraine, it's called "Kol Ha Olam Kulo." The Entire World.

Kol ha'olam kulo
Gesher tzar me'od
Veha'ikar lo lifached k'lal.

Everyone who participated in that reunion was profoundly moved, and it is no exaggeration to say there were huge vibrations, astounding aftershocks from that trip. Ever since then, I have been in constant touch with my town. From that small stone in the river, I am now on Facebook, communicating regularly not only with the families who hid me, but also daily with the mayor himself, Adam Bodzioch. I've made a large donation for a library of the Holocaust to be set up there, and I plan to give more to fund a Holocaust education program. They tell me that this is more difficult, as the right wing government has laws about this sort of thing. But we're carefully determining how to move forward, and even spread the concept to other areas of the country.

In September, 2021, the mayor called to invite me back to town. They want to do a celebration of Jewish culture and restore a monument to the 300 shot in 1942 that a Canadian friend had put up in the 1980s. Although I couldn't go, I asked my cousin Judy Rakowski to attend the celebration with her husband. I also created a map for the event, indicating the placement of every Jewish house and store in town in 1942.

They tell me that they don't want me to forget them. And I ask myself, however could I? That town, for all that happened to us there, is mine.

Chapter 35

Have You Ever Been Uncomfortable Speaking Out?

The short answer is no. I have always been very outspoken. Let me give you an example. When I was living in Canton in early 1995, I received a formal invitation to the fiftieth anniversary celebration of the liberation of Sachenhausen. It was the American ambassador to Germany who invited me. I wanted to represent the Jewish population of the camp, so I went.

So April came around, and there I was, attending this big assembly in Germany. I was glad to see that there were a number of Jews there, including a cantor, some people from Los Angeles, and a whole Israeli contingent. Lots of people. And yet, as I listened to the speeches, I realized that the group in charge had no idea that there had been Jews at the camp. After Kristallnacht in November 1938, the German sent many Jews to Sachsenhausen, but then they expelled them all in 1942. There were no Jews in the camp until our group came along a few years later, and there was quite an uproar about letting us in.

So there we were, at this big gathering, and no one was recognizing our suffering. It was really getting to me. I turned to some of the Jews there and I said, "Okay, this is ridiculous. I'm going to talk about it." I started to move closer to the main stage, to talk to someone in charge.

Then one of the survivors from L.A. said to me, "Sam, let me do it. I know you know what to say, but I speak German." And this guy got the go-ahead to talk about the Jews at the camp. To educate people. It didn't have to be me. I was just glad it got done.

Well, the president of the Sachsenhausen Museum at the time was a Mr. Ginter. After that celebration, I got very friendly with him. I used to say, "If you invite me to an event, the people in charge have to be careful." I said it half in jest, but he knew what I meant.

"You know," I told him one time, "of all the camps, Sachsenhausen was the Cadillac camp. It was so clean and orderly." He took that very nicely.

After that, Bilha and I were always invited to the Sachsenhausen anniversary events in Potsdam.

One year, the Brandenburg state president invited one hundred survivors of the camp to his house. Once again, there were speeches, and once again they recognized the French, the Kazakhs, the Poles—but there was nothing about the Jews.

I got to talking with an Israeli group.

"Nu?" I said. "Don't you think someone should say something about us?"

To my astonishment, these Israelis shook their heads. "Look, Sam," they said, "they didn't invite us to speak; we're not going to speak."

I couldn't believe my ears. But I didn't argue. Instead, I got to talking with the secretary to the President.

"Excuse me," I said, "but does the President speak English?"

"Yes, sir, he does," the man replied.

"Do you mind if I speak to him for a moment?"

The secretary was clearly surprised, but I guess he couldn't see any reason why not. He brought me over to the President, who shook my hand in a distracted manner. I understood. After all, he was doing a lot of that sort of thing that day.

"Mr. President," I said. "I would like you to say something about the Jewish people who suffered and died at the camp."

He immediately began to hem and haw. I don't think he was so against the idea in principle; he just couldn't see the reason for it.

"Well. . . . " I could see he was uncomfortable. "I did talk about the Poles, and I did talk about. . . . " I let him finish his sentence, although I wasn't really listening. I had heard it all before.

When he was finished, I said, "With all due respect, Mr. President, the Jews are special. We're a separate group. It would mean a lot, not only to the people here, but to history."

After that, I think he understood. He told his secretary to bring over the woman in charge of protocol. When he explained the situation to her, she turned to me.

"What do you want me to do, exactly?"

"Just give me the microphone, and I will talk. Of course I don't know German," I told her, "so I would like you to translate."

"Wait here," she said. "I'll get someone who can do it better that I."

When I was called up to the microphone, I looked into the eyes of not only the goyim, but the Jews as well.

"We are here," I told the crowd. We suffered. It's important that the world knows this." I was very outspoken, not willing to pull any punches. This was necessary, and clearly no one else was going to do it.

For a long time, I went to these events every April as the guest of the Museum. I met many dignitaries. Each time, I spoke about the special barracks for the Jews, number 38. One year some neo-Nazis burned down number 38 in protest of the visit of the Israeli Prime Minister Yitzhak Rabin, but the government decided to rebuild it.

For the opening of the barracks, they sent a professor to Ohio to interview me. Naturally I attended that event, as well.

I am proud of what I did. But the thing that moved me the most was that the young people taking care of the survivors at these things have always been so helpful, so understanding. Ginter's niece has been especially kind to me. One year a Jew from L.A.—he was ninety-three years old—told me he was amazed by the thoughtfulness of the young woman assigned to assist him.

"Do you think she'll go to bed with me?" he asked with a wink.

"Even if she would," I said, "What would you do with her?"

This year, the event was virtual, and once again, I was there. I will be there as long as I can. I am proud to serve as a witness.

Chapter 36

What Is Your Proudest Achievement?

That's an easy one. I've done a number of things in my life that make me proud, and I've been honored many times by wonderful organizations. I've served as president of my temple and been very active in the Jewish community in other ways, as well. But without question, the best thing I've done is to have a great family. My wife and I have been together seventy-two years, and I've been proud to support her through her own many accomplishments, such as her work as head of a Sunday school and Jewish Federation. We have three beautiful children. We've hosted many *simchas*, including our fiftieth anniversary celebration and the wedding of our daughter Tamar, who was born in Israel in 1950. Tamar is a distinguished professor and chairs the Department of Disability and Human Development at the University of Illinois at Chicago. Her husband Uri is a psychologist, and they have two beautiful children, Talya, who works with children, and Natalya, who has a job in television. And Talya has a daughter Brooklyn—all in the Chicago area.

As for David, born in 1954, he graduated from Boston University and is a very successful businessman in San Carlos, California. He and his wife Susan have two children, Erik, a musician and composer, and Elana, married to Sara.

Born in 1961 with cerebral palsy, our youngest, Daphnae, has suffered throughout her life and now lives in a group home in Chicago.

Despite living in three widely distant states, we are all very close emotionally. I'm also close with my cousin Rela Feldman, whose father, my Uncle Isaac, survived on Schindler's List, and mother—my mother's sister—survived Bergen Belsen. Rela has five children and well over a dozen grandchildren, all in Teaneck, New Jersey, or in Israel.

It may be obvious that having lost so many family members, family means everything to me, as it does to most survivors I talk to. But there's something else, too. I was born in a town where members of my family had lived for five generations. Literally dozens of relatives were within walking distance. To me, this was perfectly normal, although I know today it may seem strange. So to me, the norm is to have family around.

Finally, there were many times in my early life when I didn't know whom to trust, who would support me and who would be a source of betrayal. But I could always count on my family members. Again, I know that's not true for everyone. But for both Bilha and me, our families have always been our primary sources of hope, joy, and love.

Chapter 37

What Do You Think Sustained You during Your Darkest Days?

Survival during the Holocaust was to a great extent a matter of luck. Due to my age and health, I was sent to a work camp rather than a death house. Also lucky was the fact that I was young, but not too young. And unlike my brother, I took after my father's side of the family, who were tough, strong people, both in body and spirit. In the camps, I never had to go to the clinic. When I learned that my brother died of typhus right before the end of the war, it came as no great surprise. He had always been weaker than I. You also never knew when you were picked to do something what it was you were picked to do. And you never knew how someone in power was going to react to anything. If a commandant was having a bad day and you were in the way, that could be the end for you.

But I think that most important of all was my attitude. People were always spreading rumors of horrors: in the Ghetto, in our camp, in other camps. I came from a family of practical people, who were not overly emotional. So I did my best not to listen to the rumors. My rule was always: Why should I die today in fear of tomorrow? In other words, instead of worrying about what might be, I always had hope. All my energy went into keeping body and soul together to make it through another day. And when our tormentors treated us like field rats, a little voice inside reminded me, "Look! We are the real human beings in this hell." I found comfort in these positive thoughts.

One of my father's first cousins, Benjamin Rakowski, was chief kapo in Treblinka until he helped organize the revolt. He had a lot of enemies, and someone turned him in. I admire him, but that wasn't the kind of man I was. I resisted in my own way, not with arms, but with my heart. And I always will.

Thank you for listening.

Afterword

March 20, 2022. The U.S. Holocaust Memorial Museum held its annual gala at the fancy Boca West Country Club, just miles from Sam and Bilha's home in Boca Raton. After two years of Covid isolation, the 400 survivors, family, friends and dignitaries were eager to reconnect. The Rons, who along with their family had been instrumental in the Museum's founding and survival, were the event's honorary chairs.

At one point in the evening, a short film about Sam's extraordinary Holocaust journey was shown. Then the Rons took the stage. First, Sam made an impassioned speech. Bilha next led the audience in the song sung by the students years earlier in her husband's hometown. *The entire world is a very narrow bridge, and the main thing is not to be afraid at all.*

As the couple returned to their table, a thin, elderly man with black glasses and a white boutonniere approached. Reaching out to hug Sam, he cried, "You are my brother!"

It took a moment or two. And then it came to him. Jack Waksal. The fellow teenaged prisoner and friend who worked alongside him in Pionki, sometimes shoveling coal for twenty-four hours at a stretch. For seventy-nine years, the two men hadn't known if the other was dead or alive. Now they lived less than fifty miles apart. At one point Waksal had lived, like Sam, in Ohio, but he returned to Poland. Now ninety-seven, both men devoted much of their lives to Holocaust education. But unlike Sam, this was Jack Waksal's first Museum gala.

Since then, the two have chatted on the phone for hours. It was that first hug, however, that said everything that needed to be said.

We lived to tell the story.

The End

Glossary of Yiddish and Hebrew Terms

Balagan: Chaos, uproar (Hebrew)

Bimah: Stage at the front of a synagogue or temple (Hebrew)

Bubbe: Grandmother

Challah: Egg-based bread for the Sabbath holidays and special occasions, often braided

Cheder: Religious school, generally for boys only

Chevrei: Friends (Hebrew)

Cholent: Bean, meat, and potato-based stew, prepared prior to the Sabbath and kept warm in communal ovens or by other means to eat for Sabbath lunch

Davening: Praying

Eretz Yisrael: The Land of Israel prior to 1948 (Hebrew)

Goyim: Literally "nations," denotes non-Jews

Kibitz: Chat, often playfully

Macher: VIP

Mandelbrot: Mandel bread, Jewish biscotti

Matzoh: Unleavened bread, traditionally eaten on the holiday of Passover

Mazel tov: Congratulations (literally "good luck")

Mazkir: Director (Hebrew)

Mishigas: Craziness

Nachas: Pride

Nu: So?

Rynek: Marketplace

Shondeh: Shame

Shtetl: Small pre-World War II town in Eastern Europe with a large Jewish population

Shul: Synagogue

Simcha: Celebration

Vez iz mir: Woe is me

Yarmulke: Traditional Jewish head covering

About the Author

Samuel M. Ron is a ninety-eight-year-old survivor of the Nazi Holocaust. Born Shmuel Rakowski in Kazimierza-Wielka, Poland, he survived four concentration camps. After the war, he helped relocate Jewish orphans to the Land of Israel and served in the Haganah military force before becoming a successful builder and developer in Akron and Canton, Ohio. Mr. Ron has volunteered to speak about his experiences at hundreds of venues, including Jewish Federations in Harrisburg, Pennsylvania, Canton, Ohio, and Boca Raton, Florida; the U.S. Holocaust Memorial Museum in Washington, D.C., the March of the Living Program in Israel and Poland, Sachenhausen, Germany, and a variety of schools, libraries, synagogues and organizations in Ohio, Illinois and Palm Beach County. Mr. Ron has been featured in *the Washington Post* and on three major TV networks. His awards include the Elie Wiesel Award from the U.S. Holocaust Memorial Museum, and he was nominated for a CNN Heroes award and for Volunteer of the Year for the State of Florida. He is married to Bilha Zehori Ron, and together they have three children, four grandchildren and one great-grandchild.

Caren Schnur Neile, Ph.D., MFA, has published six books, including *Peninnah's World: A Jewish Life in Stories* (Hamilton Books). She co-founded the international academic journal *Storytelling, Self, Society*, is a columnist for the *Florida Jewish Journal*, and appears weekly on public radio WLRN. Dr. Neile has taught storytelling studies for over two decades at Florida Atlantic University and overseas as a Fulbright Senior Specialist. She has performed or lectured in seven countries and ten states.